S0-ACG-702

Atlantis and the Lost Lands

Atlantis and the Lost Lands

by Roy Stemman

Aldus Books London

Series Coordinator: John Mason
Design Director: Günter Radtke
Picture Editor: Peter Cook
Editor: Mary Senechal
Copy Editor: Maureen Cartwright
Research: Sarah Waters
General Consultant: Beppie Harrison

EDITORIAL CONSULTANTS:

COLIN WILSON
DR. CHRISTOPHER EVANS

SBN 490 00343 5
© 1976 Aldus Books Limited London
First published in the United Kingdom
in 1976 by Aldus Books Limited
17 Conway Street, London W1P 6BS
D. L. S.S.: 316/76
Printed and bound in Spain
by TONSA San Sebastián
and RONER Madrid

**Frontispiece: the biblical flood drowns the world.
Above: Plato, originator of the Atlantis legend.**

Atlantis and the Lost Lands

What is the truth about the legendary lost lands of Atlantis, Lemuria, and Mu? Did they really exist, or are they simply ideal continents of the mind? And what exactly do we know about the mysterious lost civilizations of Polynesia, Malekula, or even Easter Island? Here are some of the answers.

Contents

1

The Atlantis Mystery

Of all the world's unsolved mysteries, Atlantis is probably the biggest. Said to have been a huge island continent with an extraordinary civilization, situated in the Atlantic Ocean, it is reported to have vanished from the face of the earth in a day and a night. So complete was this devastation that Atlantis sank beneath the sea, taking with it every trace of its existence. Despite this colossal vanishing trick, the lost continent of Atlantis has exerted a mysterious influence over the human race for thousands of years. It is almost as though a primitive memory of the glorious days of Atlantis lingers on in the deepest recesses of the

Right: Italian Renaissance sculpture of Atlas supporting the earth. The Greeks had long used the Atlas myth to explain how the earth kept its place in the heavens, when Plato incorporated Atlas in his account of the fabulous empire of Atlantis. According to Plato, Atlas was the first king of Atlantis, and the kingdom derived its name from him.

7

"Atlantis our dream of a once golden past"

human mind. The passage of time has not diminished interest in the fabled continent, nor have centuries of skepticism by scientists succeeded in banishing Atlantis to obscurity in its watery grave. Thousands of books and articles have been written about the lost continent. It has inspired the authors of novels, short stories, poems, and movies. Its name has been used for ships, restaurants, magazines, and even a region of the planet Mars. Atlantean societies have been formed to theorize and speculate about the great lost land. Atlantis has come to symbolize our dream of a once golden past. It appeals to our nostalgic longing for a better, happier world; it feeds our hunger for knowledge of mankind's true origins; and above all it offers the challenge of a genuinely sensational detective story.

Today the search for evidence of the existence of Atlantis continues with renewed vigor, using 20th-century man's most sophisticated tools in the hope of discovering the continent that is said to have disappeared around 11,600 years ago. Did Atlantis exist, or is it just a myth? Ours may be the generation that finally solves this tantalizing and ancient enigma.

Atlantis is said to have been the nearest thing to paradise that the earth has seen. Fruits and vegetables grew in abundance in its rich soil. Fragrant flowers and herbs bloomed on the wooded slopes of its many beautiful mountains. All kinds of tame and wild animals roamed its meadows and magnificent forests, and drank from its rivers and lakes. Underground streams of wonderfully sweet water were used to irrigate the soil, to provide hot and cold fountains and baths for all the inhabitants—there were even baths for the horses. The earth was rich in precious metals, and the Atlanteans were wealthier than any people before or after them. Their temples and public buildings were lavishly decorated with gold, silver, brass, tin, and ivory, and their principal royal palace was a marvel of size and beauty. Besides being skilled metallurgists, the Atlanteans were accomplished engineers. A huge and complex system of canals and bridges linked their capital city with the sea and the surrounding countryside, and there were magnificent docks and harbors for the fleets of vessels that carried on a flourishing trade with overseas countries.

Whether they lived in the city or the country, the people of Atlantis had everything they could possibly want for their comfort and happiness. They were a gentle, wise, and loving people, unaffected by their great wealth, and prizing virtue above all things. In time, however, their noble nature became debased. No longer satisfied with ruling their own great land of plenty, they set about waging war on others. Their vast armies swept through the Strait of Gibraltar into the Mediterranean region, conquering large areas of North Africa and Europe. The Atlanteans were poised to strike against Athens and Egypt when the Athenian army rose up, drove them back to Gibraltar, and defeated them. Hardly had the Athenians tasted victory when a terrible cataclysm wiped out their entire army in a single day and night, and caused Atlantis to sink forever beneath the waves. Perhaps a few survivors were left to tell what had happened. At all events, the story is said to have been passed down through many generations until, more than 9200 years later, it was made known to the world for the first time.

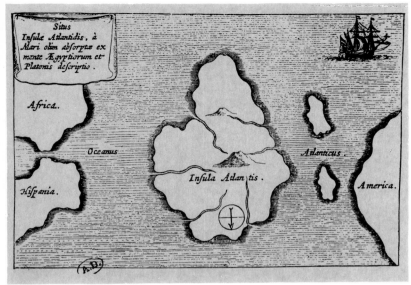

Left: map of Atlantis by the 17th-century German scholar Athanasius Kircher. Kircher based his map on Plato's description of Atlantis as an island west of the Pillars of Hercules—the Strait of Gibraltar—and situated Atlantis in the ocean that has since been named after the legendary land. Unlike modern cartographers, he placed south at the top of the map, and America appears at the right.

Below: *The Golden Age*, by 16th-century German artist Lucas Cranach. Cranach's idyllic land is very like the Atlantis of legend, a utopian country of great beauty and abundant riches, peopled by a wise and virtuous race.

The man who first committed the legend to paper was the Greek philosopher Plato, who, in about 355 B.C., wrote about Atlantis in two of his famous dialogues, the *Timaeus* and the *Critias*. Although Plato claimed that the story of the lost continent was derived from ancient Egyptian records, no such records have ever come to light, nor has any direct mention of Atlantis been found in any surviving records made before Plato's time. Every book and article on Atlantis that has ever been published has been based on Plato's account; subsequent authors have merely interpreted or added to it.

Plato was a master storyteller who put his philosophical ideas across in the form of apparently real-life events with well-known characters, and his Atlantis story might well have been firmly relegated to the realms of fiction. The very fact that it is still widely regarded as a factual account 2300 years after he wrote it shows the extraordinary power of Plato's story. It has inspired scholars to stake their reputation on the former existence of the lost continent, and explorers to go in search of its remains. Their actions were prompted not by the Greek story alone, but also by their own discoveries, which seemed to indicate that there must once have been a great landmass that acted as a bridge between our existing continents.

Why, ask the scholars, are there so many remarkable similarities between the ancient cultures of the Old and New Worlds? Why do we find the same plants and animals on continents thousands of miles apart when there is no known way for them to have been transported there? How did the primitive peoples of many lands construct technological marvels, such as Stonehenge in Britain, the huge statues of Easter Island in the Pacific, and the strange sacred cities of the Andes? Were they helped by a technically sophisticated race that has since disappeared? Above all, why do the legends of people the world over tell the same story of an overwhelming natural disaster and the arrival of godlike beings who brought with them a new culture from afar? Could the catastrophe that sank Atlantis have sent tidal waves throughout the globe, causing terrible havoc and destruction? And were the "gods" the remnants of the Atlantean race—the few survivors who were not on or near the island continent when it was engulfed?

Even without Plato's account, the quest for answers to these mysteries might have led to the belief by some in a "missing link" between the continents—a land-bridge populated by a highly evolved people in the distant past. Nevertheless, it is the Greek philosopher's story that lies at the heart of all arguments for or against the existence of such a lost continent.

Plato intended writing a trilogy in which the Atlantis story plays an important part, but he completed only one of the works, *Timaeus*, and part of the second, *Critias*. Like Plato's other writings, they take the form of dialogues or playlets in which a group of individuals discuss various political and moral issues. Leading the discussion is Plato's old teacher, the Greek philosopher Socrates. His debating companions are Timaeus, an astronomer from Italy, Critias, a poet and historian who was a distant relative of Plato, and Hermocrates, a general from Syracuse. Plato had already used the same cast of real-life

Left: Greek philosopher Plato, the first recorder of the story of Atlantis. It appears in two of the dialogues, in which Plato used actual people as mouthpieces for his own philosophical ideas. The story, set down some 2300 years ago, still fascinates and perplexes the world today. Below: *The School of Athens*, by Italian Renaissance artist Raphael, depicts the greatest thinkers of ancient Greece. Beneath the arch, Plato (left) and Aristotle talk.

characters in his most famous dialogue, *The Republic*, written some years previously, and he planned his trilogy as a sequel to that debate, in which the four men had talked at some length about ideal government.

Plato set the meeting of the four men in Critias's house in June 421 B.C. *Timaeus* begins on the day following the debate recorded in *The Republic*, and the men start by recalling their previous conversation. Then Hermocrates mentions "a story derived from ancient tradition" that Critias knows. Pressed for details, Critias recalls how, a century and a half earlier, the great Athenian statesman Solon had visited Egypt. (Solon was a real person and he did visit Egypt, although his trip took place around 590 B.C., some 20 years earlier than the date given by Plato.)

Left: according to Plato, Athenian statesman Solon was the first Greek to learn the story of Atlantis. He was told of the kingdom by priests while visiting Egypt.

Below: Greek hoplites, or foot soldiers, pictured on the Chigi vase of the 7th century B.C. Heavily armed infantrymen like these would have taken part in the war between Atlantis and Athens that, Solon was told, had heralded the empire's end. The final battle was over and Atlantis had been defeated when the world was shaken by earthquakes, and floodwater covered the land. The earth swallowed up the Athenian army, and Atlantis disappeared into the ocean depths.

Critias says that while Solon was in Sais, an Egyptian city having close ties with Athens, a group of priests told him the story of Atlantis—"a tale that, though strange, is certainly true." Solon made notes of the conversation, and intended recording the story for posterity, but he did not do so. Instead he told it to a relative, Dropides, who passed it on to his son, Critias the elder, who eventually told his grandson, another Critias—the man who features in Plato's dialogues.

In *Timaeus* Critias gives a brief account of what the priests had told Solon. According to ancient Egyptian records there had been a great Athenian empire 9000 years earlier (that is, in about 9600 B.C.). At the same time there had been a mighty empire of Atlantis based on an island or continent west of the Pillars of Hercules (the Strait of Gibraltar) that was larger than North Africa and Asia Minor combined. Beyond it lay a chain of islands that stretched across the ocean to another huge continent.

The Atlanteans ruled over their central island and several others, and over parts of the great continent on the other side of the ocean. Then their armies struck eastward into the Mediterranean region, conquering North Africa as far as Egypt and southern Europe up to the Greek borders. "This vast power, gathered into one, endeavored to subdue at one blow our country and yours," said the Egyptian priests, "and the whole of the region within the strait. . . ." Athens, standing alone, defeated the Atlanteans. "But afterward there occurred violent earthquakes and floods; and in a single day and night of destruction all your warlike men in a body sank into the earth, and the island of Atlantis in like manner disappeared in the depths of the sea. For which reason the sea in those parts is impassable and impenetrable, because there is so much shallow mud in the way, caused by the subsidence of the island."

Socrates is delighted with Critias's story, which has "the very great advantage of being a fact and not a fiction." However, the rest of *Timaeus* is taken up with a discourse on science, and the story of Atlantis is continued in Plato's next dialogue, the *Critias*, where Critias gives a much fuller description of the island continent. He goes back to the island's very beginning when the gods were apportioned parts of the earth, as is usual in ancient histories. Poseidon, Greek god of the sea and also of earthquakes, was given Atlantis, and there he fell in love with a mortal maiden called Cleito. Cleito dwelled on a hill in Atlantis, and to prevent anyone reaching her home, Poseidon encircled the hill with alternate rings of land and water, "two of land and three of water, which he turned as with a lathe." He also laid on abundant supplies of food and water to the hill, "bringing up two springs of water from beneath the earth, one of warm water and the other of cold, and making every variety of food to spring up abundantly from the soil."

Poseidon and Cleito produced 10 children—five pairs of male twins—and Poseidon divided Atlantis and its adjacent islands among these 10 sons to rule as a confederacy of kings. The first-born of the eldest twins, Atlas (after whom Atlantis was named), was made chief king. The kings in turn had numerous children, and their descendants ruled for many generations.

As the population of Atlantis grew and developed, the people

Above: men of Crete bringing tribute to the Egyptians, an Egyptian wall-painting of the 15th century B.C. At that time, a great civilization flourished on Crete— a civilization that had trading links with Egypt and other Mediterranean lands. By the time Solon visited Egypt, some 900 years later, the Cretan civilization had fallen. But could it have been Egyptian accounts of Crete that gave rise to the Atlantis myth?

Above: Poseidon, Greek god of the sea and, according to Plato, the founder of Atlantis. Legend tells how, when the Greek gods divided the earth at the beginning of the world, Poseidon was given the island of Atlantis. There, he fell in love with Cleito, a mortal, who bore him 10 sons. Poseidon divided Atlantis and its islands among his sons, who ruled as a confederacy of kings. The chief king, however, was the eldest son Atlas, who gave his name to the land he ruled.

accomplished great feats of engineering and architecture. They built palaces and temples, harbors and docks, and reaped the rich harvest of their agricultural and mineral resources. The kings and their descendants built the city of Atlantis around Cleito's hill on the southern coast of the island continent. It was a circular city, about 11 miles in diameter, and Cleito's hill, surrounded by its concentric rings of land and water, formed a citadel about three miles in diameter, situated at the very center of the impressive city.

The kings built bridges to connect the land rings, and tunnels through which ships could pass from one ring of water to the next. The rings of land were surrounded by stone walls plated with precious metals, and another wall ran around the entire city.

The outermost ring of water became a great harbor, crowded with shipping.

A huge canal, 300 feet wide and 100 feet deep, linked the great harbor with the sea at the southern end, and joined the city to a vast irrigated plain, sheltered by lofty mountains, which lay beyond the city walls in the north. This rectangular plain, measuring 230 by 340 miles, was divided into 60,000 square lots, assigned to farmers. The mountains beyond housed "many wealthy villages of country folk, and rivers, and lakes, and meadows, supplying food for every animal, wild or tame, and much wood of various sorts, abundant for each and every kind of work." The inhabitants of the mountains and of the rest of the country were "a vast multitude having leaders to whom they were assigned according to their dwellings and villages." These leaders and the farmers on the plain were each required to supply men for the Atlantean army, which included light and heavy infantry, cavalry, and chariots.

Plato and Critias paint a vivid picture of Atlantean engineering and architecture with an attention to detail that bears the hallmark of a very factual account. Critias tells how the stone used for the city's buildings was quarried from beneath the central island (Cleito's hill) and from beneath the outer and inner circles of land. "One kind of stone was white, another black, and a third red, and as they quarried they at the same time hollowed out docks within, having roofs formed of the native rock. Some of their buildings were simple, but in others they put together different stones, which they intermingled for the sake of ornament, to be a natural source of delight." But it was into their magnificent temples that the Atlanteans poured their greatest artistic and technical skills. In the center of the citadel was a holy temple dedicated to Cleito and Poseidon and this was surrounded by an enclosure of gold. Nearby stood Poseidon's own temple, a superb structure covered in silver, with pinnacles of gold. The roof's interior was covered with ivory, and lavishly decorated with gold, silver, and *orichalc*—probably a fine grade of brass or bronze—which "glowed like fire." Inside the temple was a massive gold statue of Poseidon driving a chariot drawn by six winged horses and surrounded by 100 sea nymphs on dolphins. This was so high that its head touched the temple roof. Gold statues of Atlantis's original 10 kings and their wives stood outside the temple.

Critias tells of the beautiful buildings that were constructed around the warm and cold fountains in the center of the city. Trees were planted between the buildings, and cisterns were designed—some open to the heavens, others roofed over—to be used as baths. "There were the kings' baths, and the baths of private persons, which were kept apart; and there were separate baths for women, and for horses and cattle, and to each of them they gave as much adornment as was suitable. Of the water that ran off they carried some to the grove of Poseidon, where were growing all manner of trees of wonderful height and beauty, owing to the excellence of the soil, while the remainder was conveyed by aqueducts along the bridges to the outer circles; and there were many temples built and dedicated to many gods; also gardens and places of exercise, some for men, and others for

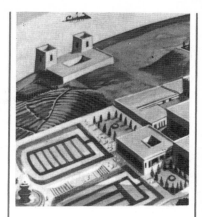

Plato's Atlantis

Fable or fact? The truth about Plato's Atlantis remains obscure to this day. The dialogue in which the Greek philosopher described the city was never completed, so it is impossible to know whether Plato based his description on a real country or created an imaginary land to illustrate his philosophical ideas. Whether or not Atlantis ever existed, Plato's account is so detailed that it can be used to reconstruct the city he described.

Poseidon surrounded the hill where his beloved Cleito dwelt by concentric rings of land and water, and the Atlanteans made these an integral part of the city they built around Cleito's hill. Tunnels beneath the land rings enabled ships to sail into the heart of the city and from the outermost ring of water they could pass through a wide canal to the Atlantic beyond. Bridges linked the city with the land rings.

In the city itself, the Atlanteans constructed a fabulous temple dedicated to Poseidon and a palace "a marvel to behold." Temple, palace, and the surrounding buildings were ornamented with gold and silver, brass, tin, ivory, and *orichalc*—probably bronze. Trees encircled the buildings, and magnificent parks and gardens surrounded the warm and cold fountains Poseidon had made.

horses in both of the two islands formed by the zones [rings of water]; and in the center of the larger of the two there was set apart a racecourse of a stadium [about 607 feet] in width, and in length allowed to extend all around the island, for horses to race in."

At alternate intervals of five and six years the 10 kings of Atlantis met in the temple of Poseidon to consult on matters of government and to administer justice. During this meeting a strange ritual was enacted. After offering up prayers to the gods, the kings were required to hunt bulls, which roamed freely within the temple, and to capture one of them for sacrifice, using only staves and nooses. The captured animal was led to a bronze column in the temple, on which the laws of Atlantis were inscribed, and was slain so that its blood ran over the sacred inscription. After further ceremony, the kings partook of a banquet and when darkness fell they wrapped themselves in beautiful dark-blue robes. Sitting in a circle they gave their judgments, which were recorded at daybreak on tablets of gold.

In the course of time, the people of Atlantis began to lose the love of wisdom and virtue that they had inherited from Poseidon. As their divine nature was diluted and human nature got the upper hand, they became greedy, corrupt, and domineering. Whereupon, says Plato, "Zeus, the god of gods, who rules by law, and is able to see into such things, perceiving that an honorable race was in a most wretched state, and wanting to punish them that they might be chastened and improve, collected all the gods into his most holy abode, which, being placed in the

center of the universe, sees all things that partake of generation. And when he had called them together he spoke as follows. . . ."

And there, enigmatically and frustratingly, Plato's story of Atlantis breaks off, never to be completed. Some scholars regard the *Critias* dialogue as a rough draft that Plato abandoned. Others assume he intended to continue the story in the third part of his trilogy, but he never even started that work. He went on, instead, to write his last dialogue, *The Laws*.

Controversy has raged over Plato's story ever since he wrote it, 2300 years ago. Was his account fact, part-fact, or total fiction? Each explanation has its adherents, and each has been hotly defended over the centuries. Plato's story certainly presents a number of problems. Critics of the Atlantis theory claim that these invalidate the story as a factual account. Supporters maintain that they can be accepted as poetic license, exaggeration, or understandable mistakes that have crept in during the telling and retelling of the story over many centuries before Plato reported it.

The greatest stumbling block is the date that the Greek philosopher gives for the destruction of Atlantis. The Egyptian priests are said to have told Solon that Atlantis was destroyed 9000 years before his visit, in about 9600 B.C., which is far earlier than any known evidence of civilization. Supporters of Atlantis point out that modern discoveries are constantly pushing back the boundaries of human prehistory and we may yet discover that civilization is far older than we think. However, Plato makes it clear that in 9600 B.C. Athens was also the home of a mighty civilization that defeated the Atlanteans. Archaeologists claim

Above: rhyton or ritual pouring vessel in the shape of a bull's head found during the excavation of the palace of Knossos, Crete. Arthur Evans' excavations on Crete proved that the bull had held as important a place in the actual life of ancient Crete as that accorded it by Greek legend. His discoveries suggested the possibility of a factual basis for other ancient myths. Had the Minotaur actually existed? Was there a Cretan labyrinth? Could the island of Crete be the Atlantis of legendary fame?

that their knowledge of Greece in the early days of its development is sufficiently complete to rule out the possibility of highly developed people in that country as early as 9600 B.C. Their evidence suggests that either Plato's story is an invention or he has the date wrong.

Assuming that Plato's facts are right but his date wrong, what evidence do we have to support his account of the origin of the Atlantis story? Bearing in mind that the war was principally between Atlantis and Athens, it seems odd that there were no Greek records of the battle, and that the account should have originated in Egypt. However, Plato has an explanation for this. The Egyptian priests are said to have told Solon that a series of catastrophes had destroyed the Greek records, whereas their own had been preserved. The problem here is that if the Egyptian records existed at the time of Solon's visit, they have since disappeared as completely as Atlantis itself.

Supposing that Solon did hear about Atlantis during his Egyptian trip, is it credible that such a detailed story could have been passed down through the generations as Plato asks us to believe? This is not impossible, because the art of accurate oral transmission was highly developed in the ancient world. Moreover, Solon is said to have taken notes of his conversation with the priests, and Critias claims that these were handed down to his relatives. However, here again we encounter a difficulty. For whereas in one place Critias states that he is still in possession of Solon's notes, in another he declares that he lay awake all night ransacking his memory for details of the Atlantis story that his grandfather had told him. Why didn't he simply refresh his memory from Solon's notes? And why didn't he show the notes to his three companions as incontrovertible proof of the truth of his rather unlikely story?

Yet another problem is that Plato dates the meeting of Socrates, Timaeus, Critias, and Hermocrates, during which Atlantis is discussed, as 421 B.C. Plato may have been present during their conversation, but as he was only six years old at the

20

time, he could hardly have taken in much of their discussion, let alone made detailed notes of it. Either his account is based on records made by someone else, or the date is wrong, or this part of his story at least is an invention.

Critics of the Atlantis story believe that it is simply a myth invented to put across the great philosopher's views on war and corruption. Plato used real people in his other dialogues, and put his words into their mouths, too, as a dramatic device to present his ideas. There is no reason, say the detractors, to assume that *Timaeus* and *Critias* are different in this respect. But Plato seems to expect his readers to draw different conclusions. He is at great pains to stress the truth of his account, tracing it back to Solon, a highly respected statesman with a reputation for being "straight-tongued," and having Critias declare that the Atlantis story, "though strange, is certainly true." And why, if his sole intention was to deliver a philosophical treatise, did Plato fill his account with remarkable detail and then stop abruptly at the very point where we would expect the "message" to be delivered? In spite of the errors and contradictions that have found their

way into Plato's account, his story of Atlantis can still be viewed as an exciting recollection of previously unrecorded events.

History certainly provides us with other examples of supposedly mythical places subsequently being discovered. Around 850 B.C.—500 years before Plato wrote of Atlantis—another great Greek, Homer, wrote two epic poems, the *Iliad* and the *Odyssey*. Homer's poems record the stories of the heroes of Mycenae, which had been handed down by bards over the centuries. In the *Iliad* he deals with just a few days of the Greeks' 10-year siege of Troy, and in the *Odyssey* he describes the wanderings of Odysseus as he returns home to the island of Ithaca after the Trojan War. These events had occurred several centuries before Homer wrote of them, and although the Greeks never doubted the truth of these brilliant works, European scholars dismissed them as pure fantasy. There were sufficient mistakes in them for the skeptics to hold them up to ridicule as factual stories.

Then in 1871 the German archaeologist Heinrich Schliemann excavated in Hissarlik in northwestern Turkey, and uncovered Troy exactly where Homer had situated it. Subsequent research has shown that Homer's accounts were based on real events. As the Irish scholar J. V. Luce observes in his book *The End of Atlantis*: "Classical scholars laughed at Schliemann when he set out with Homer in one hand and a spade in the other. But he dug up Troy, and thereby demonstrated that it is rash to underestimate the historical value of folk memory. Sir Arthur Evans did much the same thing when he found the labyrinthine home of the Minotaur at Knossos." Indeed, Sir Arthur Evans revealed that a highly advanced European civilization had flourished on the island of Crete long before the time of Homer, some 4500 years ago.

This should be justification enough to keep an open mind on Plato's account. The problem is that whereas Troy and Knossos were simply buried, Atlantis could be submerged hundreds or even thousands of feet beneath the waves. And the force of the destruction may have destroyed the remains beyond recognition. However, if Plato's account is based on fact, then we know that the Atlanteans traded with their neighbors. In this case there should be some evidence of their influence and culture in lands that survived the catastrophe. Believers in Atlantis have furnished us with a formidable array of such "proofs." Certainly there are enough puzzling architectural and technical achievements scattered around the globe to lend support to the idea of a highly advanced, Atlantean-type civilization that was responsible.

Although Plato appears to place Atlantis in the Atlantic Ocean, and early cartographers did likewise, numerous scholars and other Atlantis enthusiasts have since scoured the globe for more likely sites. Surprisingly, these have not always been in the ocean. The lost kingdom of Atlantis has been "found" at various times in the Pacific Ocean, the North Sea, the Sahara Desert, Sweden, southern Spain, Palestine, Cyprus, Crete, the West Indies, and Peru, to name but a few.

Inevitably, with a lack of physical evidence of Atlantis, the occultists have been busy for centuries producing a wealth of information about the lost civilization. They believe that the past is accessible to properly attuned psychics, who can delve

Above: Arthur Evans in 1907, a few years after he had made the archaeological discoveries in Crete that won him world-wide fame.

Right: one of a number of reconstructions made by Evans to show how the palace of Knossos must have looked in the heyday of Minoan civilization. The culture Evans discovered was distinguished by the beauty and originality of its art and architecture, and by the comfort and prosperity that its people seem to have enjoyed.

Above: the throne room of the palace of Knossos in Crete. At the beginning of this century, British archaeologist Arthur Evans discovered in Knossos the remains of a previously unknown civilization contemporary with that of Mycenae in mainland Greece. Evans named the civilization Minoan after the legendary Minos of Crete. Just as Schliemann had at Hissarlik, Evans proved by his discoveries at Knossos that a legend had its basis in historical fact.

into history and see events happening clairvoyantly. Using such methods a number of individuals have produced vivid descriptions of life on Atlantis. Some merely expanded Plato's account. Others gave descriptions so astonishing that it can only be presumed that they were tuning in to some other lost civilization than the one immortalized by Plato. In the 1890s, for example, the English occultist W. Scott-Elliot used astral clairvoyance to reveal that Atlantis occupied most of what is now the Atlantic, more than one million years ago. It was inhabited by warrior tribes, including Rmoahals, black aboriginals who stood 10 to 12 feet tall. The ruling race, Scott-Elliot reported, were the Toltecs, who, though only eight feet tall, made slaves of the Rmoahals. Some 200,000 years ago groups of Toltecs emigrated to Egypt and Mexico as well as visiting England. The rulers of Atlantis then took to black magic, and suffered retribution in the form of earthquake and flood, but the emigrants were safe in their new homelands.

Another seer who added to the literature on Atlantis was Edgar Cayce, the famous American clairvoyant prophet and psychic healer who died in 1945. While in a deep trance Cayce gave thousands of "psychic interviews" concerning the supposed previous incarnations of his clients. According to Cayce some of his clients were former Atlanteans, and in describing their lives he added fascinating details of the great civilization. These include references to the Atlanteans' use of what seem to be lasers and masers, described by Cayce in 1942, many years before modern scientists had developed them.

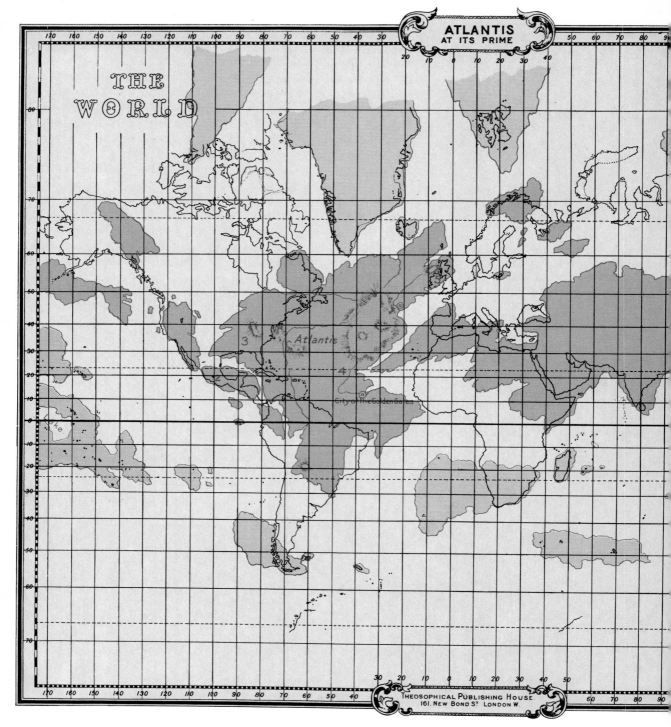

ATLANTIS
AT ITS PRIME

THEOSOPHICAL PUBLISHING HOUSE
161. NEW BOND ST. LONDON W.

THE WORLD

Above: British occultist W. Scott-Elliot's map of Atlantis "at its prime." The Atlantis myth, unsupported by factual evidence, has been particularly prone to exploitation by those claiming communion with supernatural powers. According to Scott-Elliot, he learned about Atlantis through astral clairvoyance, which had revealed to him the configurations of the earth's landmasses prior to that existing today. The land of Atlantis, he stated, had appeared toward the end of the Mesozoic era and had occupied most of what is now the Atlantic. Populated in turn by various races, each of which was described in detail, Scott-Elliot's Atlantis survived until about 800,000 years ago.

24

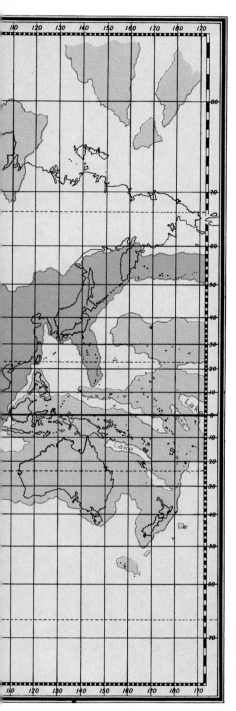

The gist of the many Cayce writings dealing with Atlantis is that the Atlanteans were technically as advanced as we are, and it was the tremendous energies that they developed—possibly nuclear—which brought about their destruction. Many people laugh at Cayce, just as they scoff at Plato's story, but the seer's followers expect to have the last laugh. They believe the earth has begun to undergo major upheavals that will cause large parts of Atlantis to rise again from the sea. In 1940 Cayce predicted that these changes would start around 1968 and 1969, when part of the "western section of Atlantis" would reappear near the Bahamas. Strangely enough, in 1968 a number of underwater formations, including what appeared to be ruined buildings, were sighted off Bimini in the Bahamas. Cayce's followers claim that these "finds" are a fulfillment of the seer's prophecy, and that far more dramatic discoveries will occur over the next 30 years or so. Unfortunately Cayce also predicted that the very upheavals that would uncover the lost continent would also submerge many parts of our existing land, including most of New York City and Japan.

The mystery of Atlantis will not be solved by the study of Plato alone. Clues from a tremendous number of disciplines, and theories from the orthodox to the occult, deserve an objective appraisal. There are those who believe that the quest for the lost continent is merely an expression of mankind's need to believe in a golden age when life was idyllic and men and women were perfect. For them, Atlantis is a dream without foundation. But there are others who view man's ancient legends and mysterious monuments very differently. In their opinion our picture of evolution and civilization is totally inadequate. We choose to ignore the puzzles that do not conform to our cosy picture of development, without realizing that these very enigmas hold the key to a far greater understanding of our past.

The missing link, according to this argument, is Atlantis, and that is why the lost continent still excites such astonishing interest. Find Atlantis, they say, and everything will fall into place. And find Atlantis we may well do, for there is a growing body of people who believe from the clues so far produced that we are now on the very brink of rediscovering the lost civilization.

Left: Edgar Cayce, American clairvoyant and perhaps the most famous and successful psychic healer of all time. While in a state of trance, Cayce conducted psychic interviews with his clients, during which he often mentioned Atlantis. He revealed many fascinating facts about the lost continent and predicted that it would rise again from the sea in 1968. Although no new continent surfaced from beneath the waters in 1968, what appeared to be ruined buildings were observed off the Bahamas. Could Cayce's success as a healer be equaled by one as an archaeological seer?

2

The Quest for Atlantis

In 1912 the *New York American* published a sensational article. It was written by Dr. Paul Schliemann, grandson of Heinrich Schliemann, the man who discovered Troy. Paul Schliemann announced that he had in his possession coins and an inscribed metal plate belonging to the Atlantean culture. Here at last, it seemed, was proof of the existence of Atlantis.

In his article entitled "How I Discovered Atlantis, the Source of All Civilization," Paul Schliemann explained that the Atlantean artifacts had been left to him by his famous grandfather, who had discovered them during his excavations. Heinrich

Right: the gold mask that covered the head and shoulders of the mummified body of Tutankhamun, pharaoh of Egypt in the 14th century B.C. According to American Ignatius Donnelly, the "Father of Scientific Atlantology," ancient Egypt was an Atlantean colony, and its civilization and religion were based on those of Atlantis.

"Schliemann stated... he had solved the Atlantis mystery"

Schliemann had died before completing his search for evidence of the lost continent. However, he had left his family a sealed envelope containing a number of secret papers about Atlantis, together with an ancient, owl-headed vase. A note on the envelope warned that it should be opened only by a member of the family prepared to swear that he would devote his life to researching the matters dealt with in the papers. Paul Schliemann made that pledge and opened the envelope.

His grandfather's first instruction was to break open the owl-headed vase. Inside he found several square coins of platinum-aluminum-silver alloy and a plate made of a silverlike metal that bore the inscription, in Phoenician: "Issued in the Temple of Transparent Walls." Heinrich Schliemann's notes told of finds made on the site of Troy, including a huge bronze vase containing coins and objects made of metal, bone, and pottery. The vase and some of its contents were inscribed with the words: "From King Cronos of Atlantis."

"You can imagine my excitement," wrote the young Schliemann. "Here was the first material evidence of that great continent whose legend has lived for ages. . . ." He went on to state that, by following up these clues with his own investigations, he had finally solved the Atlantis mystery. However, his "research" would appear to have gone no further than a study of the arguments of the pro-Atlantis enthusiasts, because the rest of his article consisted of material clearly culled (without acknowledgment) from their works. Like others before him, Paul Schliemann claimed the cultures of the New and Old Worlds had a common origin in Atlantis. He said he had read the *Troano Codex*, an ancient Mayan text that until then had defied transla-

Below: Paul Schliemann's map of the possible location of Atlantis—the dark circles represent the city described by Plato. In 1912 Schliemann, grandson of the discoverer of Troy, published an article setting out what he claimed was conclusive proof of the existence of Atlantis. Most of his evidence, however, turned out to have been lifted without acknowledgment from other writers.

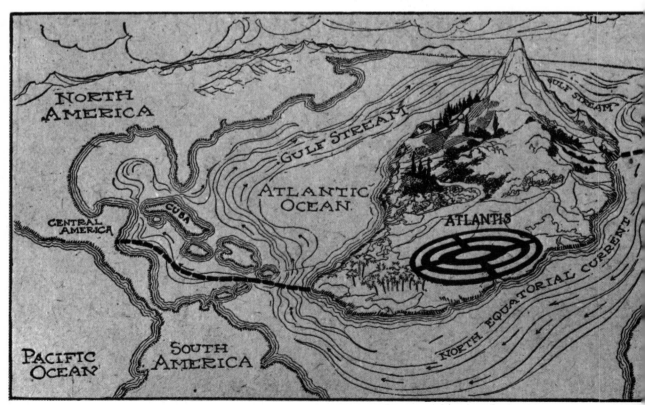

tion. It told of the sinking of an island named Mu, and he had found corroboration of this account in a 4000-year-old Chaldean manuscript from a Buddhist temple in Tibet.

It was at this point that the experts began to have misgivings. Paul Schliemann claimed to have read the *Troano Codex* in the British Museum—but it is preserved in the National Museum of Madrid. And his "translation" was remarkably similar to that made by an eccentric French scholar, which seemed to owe more to a vivid imagination than to a linguistic talent.

Schliemann promised to divulge the full story of his discoveries in a forthcoming book. Like Atlantis, the book never appeared. Nor did the vase, coins, and other precious relics ever see the light of day. Although the Schliemann story was clearly a hoax, this has not stopped the more credulous pro-Atlantists from using it to support their claims, sometimes confusing Paul with his famous grandfather to make matters worse.

This rather sad episode is typical of the numerous false leads that have bedeviled genuine attempts to uncover the truth about Atlantis. Time and again, men of apparent erudition and integrity have claimed the discovery of vital clues. Using ancient manuscripts, folklore, and legends, they have pieced together impressive "evidence" about the sinking of the island continent, the appearance of its inhabitants, what happened to the survivors, and, above all, the true site of Atlantis. Some of these theories, based on inaccurate information, have been rapidly demolished by fellow scholars. Others are so revolutionary in their implications that, if they were proved correct, the entire history of the world would need to be rewritten.

Ever since Plato's time writers, scholars, and explorers have

Below: Heinrich Schliemann's excavations at Hissarlik. Paul Schliemann claimed that his grandfather had found some objects of Atlantean origin during his excavations at Hissarlik, and that he had left these to any member of his family prepared to devote his life to the search for the lost continent. It appears, however, that the story was invented by Paul as a publicity gimmick.

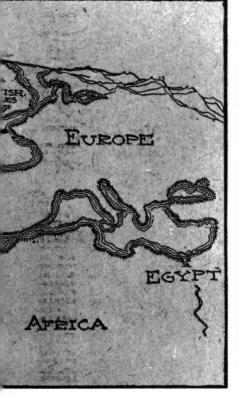

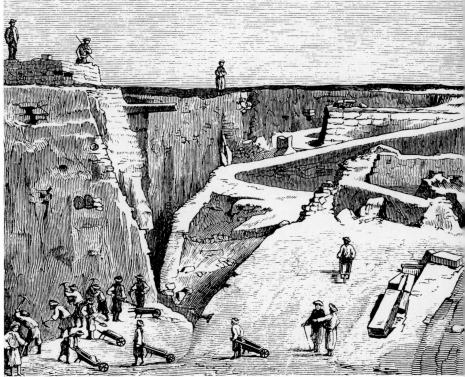

sought—and "found"—Atlantis in almost every corner of the
globe. Francis Bacon, the 17th-century English philosopher and
statesman, thought that Plato's Atlantis was America. Another
17th-century scholar, the Swede Olof Rudbeck, wrote a lengthy
treatise "proving" that Atlantis was Sweden. In the 18th century,
French astronomer Jean Bailly—a victim of the French Revolu-
tion—traced Atlantis to Spitsbergen in the Arctic Ocean.
Francis Wilford, a British officer in India in the 19th century,
was convinced that the British Isles were a remnant of the lost
continent, and his theory was enthusiastically adopted by the
poet William Blake. Other leading theorists and investigators—
some of whom have devoted their lives to the subject—have
placed Atlantis in North Africa, South Africa, Central America,
Australia, France, the North Sea, Sardinia, Israel and Lebanon,
Malta, the Sahara, East Prussia and the Baltic, Siberia, Green-
land, Iraq, Iran, Brazil, and the Pacific and Indian Oceans. The
peoples of these regions naturally had a vested interest in such
theories, because the location of Atlantis in or near their country
would give them a reasonable claim to be descended from
Atlantean survivors.

It may seem odd that most of the Atlantis theorists mentioned
above have chosen *land* areas as the site of a supposedly drowned
continent. There are a number of reasons for this, including the
obvious one that until recent times extensive underwater exploration has not been possible. Some theorists base their choice on a
reinterpretation of Plato's story, believing that he built his
account on the memory of some ancient disaster of relatively

limited proportions. Others point out that vast areas of our present landmasses were once under water; similarly, areas that are now submerged were once above sea level. According to this argument, Atlantis was submerged, as Plato said, but has since reappeared as one of the countries or areas listed. However, geological evidence does not support this theory. Most geologists agree that, although the earth's surface has undergone many major changes, these have occurred only very gradually over millions of years. As far as they are concerned, large landmasses do not rise and sink rapidly enough to account for the overnight drowning of Atlantis and its reemergence as one of our present-day land areas.

The Atlantis-seekers mentioned so far are, however, in a minority. By far the greater number of scholars who have studied the Atlantis enigma agree with Plato. If the lost continent was anywhere, they believe, it was in the Atlantic Ocean—and they have produced a wealth of material to support their case.

Of all the theorists who have placed Atlantis in the Atlantic, none has argued more persuasively or made a greater impact on the study of Atlantis than the American Ignatius T. T. Donnelly, sometimes called the Father of Scientific Atlantology. Donnelly's enormous physical and intellectual energy brought him success at an early age. Born in Philadelphia in 1831, he studied law and was admitted to the bar at the age of 22. Three years later he and his bride went to Minnesota, where Donnelly and a group of friends had purchased some land near St. Paul and hoped to found a great Middle West metropolis, Nininger City. As part of the campaign to publicize this dream, Donnelly edited and published *The Emigrant Journal*. But Nininger City was never developed, possibly because of the financial depression that occurred in the 1850s.

Instead, the chubby dynamic Donnelly turned his attention to politics, and was elected Lieutenant-Governor of Minnesota at the age of 28. Four years later he was sent to Congress, where he served for eight years. Donnelly was renowned as a brilliant, forceful, and witty speaker, and rapidly earned the respect of fellow members of the House of Representatives.

Behind the public image, however, Donnelly was experiencing a period of intense loneliness. Soon after his arrival in Washington, his wife had died, and Donnelly turned to study for solace. During his two terms as the member from Minnesota, he spent long hours in the magnificent Library of Congress, soaking up all the information he could.

After his defeat in the election of 1870, Donnelly returned to his home in the ghost town of Nininger City. There, surrounded by his notes and a large personal library, he began writing the books that were to make him famous throughout the world. After years of isolation and poverty during which he persevered with the task in hand to the exclusion of all else, Donnelly produced his masterpiece: *Atlantis, the Antediluvian World*. Published in 1882, this unique study of the lost continent became an overnight sensation. The following year another book, *Ragnarok, the Age of Fire and Gravel*, joined his first as a best seller. This dealt with the cosmic aspects of natural cataclysms such as that which supposedly submerged Atlantis. The extent

Below: 18th-century French astronomer Jean Bailly, a member of the French Academy of Sciences. Besides orthodox scientific works, Bailly wrote a book on ancient astronomy in which he claimed that Spitsbergen was Atlantis, and the source of all Asian civilizations.

of Donnelly's influence on the study of Atlantis can be judged by the enormous and continuing success of his books. His first work, for example, has been reprinted 50 times and is still in print today, nearly a century after it was written. Donnelly transformed what had been, until then, a subject of speculation mainly among intellectuals into a popular cult, and one that has survived ever since.

This giant of Atlantology did more than look for confirmation of Plato's story. He used it as the basis for a picture of Atlantis that went far beyond anything stated—or that could even have been imagined—by the Greek philosopher. His theories were distilled into 13 "theses":

"1. That there once existed in the Atlantic Ocean, opposite the mouth of the Mediterranean Sea, a large island, which was the remnant of an Atlantic continent, and known to the ancient world as Atlantis.

"2. That the description of this island given by Plato is not, as has been long supposed, fable, but veritable history.

"3. That Atlantis was the region where man first rose from a state of barbarism to civilization.

"4. That it became, in the course of ages, a populous and mighty nation, from whose overflowings the shores of the Gulf of Mexico, the Mississippi River, the Amazon, the Pacific coast of South America, the Mediterranean, the west coast of Europe and Africa, the Baltic, the Black Sea, and the Caspian were populated by civilized nations.

"5. That it was the true Antediluvian world; the Garden of Eden; the Gardens of the Hesperides; the Elysian Fields; the Gardens of Alcinous; the Mesomphales; the Olympes; the Asgard of the traditions of the ancient nations; representing a universal memory of a great land, where early mankind dwelt for ages in peace and happiness.

"6. That the gods and goddesses of the ancient Greeks, the Phoenicians, the Hindoos, and the Scandinavians were simply the kings, queens, and heroes of Atlantis; and the acts attributed to them in mythology are a confused recollection of real historical events.

"7. That the mythology of Egypt and Peru represented the original religion of Atlantis, which was sun-worship.

"8. That the oldest colony formed by the Atlanteans was probably in Egypt, whose civilization was a reproduction of that of the Atlantic island.

"9. That the implements of the 'Bronze Age' of Europe were derived from Atlantis. The Atlanteans were also the first manufacturers of iron.

"10. That the Phoenician alphabet, parent of all the European alphabets, was derived from an Atlantis alphabet, which was also conveyed from Atlantis to the Mayas of Central America.

"11. That Atlantis was the original seat of the Aryan or Indo-European family of nations, as well as of the Semitic peoples, and possibly also of the Turanian races.

"12. That Atlantis perished in a terrible convulsion of nature, in which the whole island sank into the ocean, with nearly all its inhabitants.

"13. That a few persons escaped in ships and on rafts, and

Right: Ignatius Donnelly, author of *Atlantis: the Antediluvian World*, one of the most influential books on the subject ever published. Donnelly, a man of wide-ranging interests and considerable erudition, began his career as a lawyer, subsequently emigrating to Minnesota, where he tried unsuccessfully to found a new city. Turning to politics, at 28 he became Lieutenant-Governor of Minnesota and was subsequently elected to Congress. Donnelly spent much of his free time in Washington in the Library of Congress, reading all that he could.

Below: Donnelly's library at Nininger in Minnesota, the town he had hoped to build into the greatest city of the Midwest. After his defeat in the 1870 election, Donnelly returned to Nininger and there began to write his book on Atlantis. First published in 1882, it was still in print, in its 50th edition, in 1949!

Above: cartoon representing Donnelly as Don Quixote, from the Minneapolis *Journal* of February 24, 1891. Although Donnelly was never reelected to Washington, he continued to take an active interest in politics throughout his life. He became a member of the Minnesota State Senate and twice ran—though unsuccessfully—for Vice-President of the United States.

Below: Donnelly's map of Atlantis and its empire, from *Atlantis: the Antediluvian World*. Donnelly believed that all the dark areas were colonized and civilized through contacts with Atlantis.

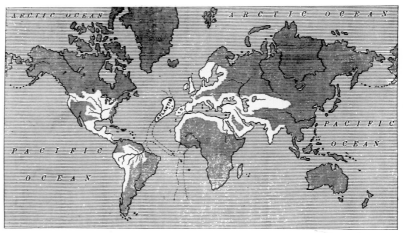

carried to the nations east and west tidings of the appalling catastrophe, which has survived to our own time in the Flood and Deluge legends of the different nations of the old and new worlds."

Donnelly, it seems, had not only "discovered" Atlantis but also succeeded in solving nearly all the mysteries of the past at the same time. He maintained that Atlantis was the source of all civilization (Plato made no such claim) and as such had inspired the myths and legends of numerous races—many of which are indeed remarkably similar.

Donnelly argued that the resemblances between many species of American and European animals and plants are due to their having a common origin—Atlantis. Quoting a number of authorities to support his case, he stated that such plants as tobacco, guava, cotton, and bananas were not confined to one hemisphere before Columbus—as was generally thought—but had long been grown in both the New and the Old World. In his view these plants must have crossed the Atlantic by means of an Atlantean land-bridge.

Donnelly also believed that the civilization of ancient Egypt emerged suddenly rather than evolving gradually over thousands

Above: the pyramids of Cheops and Khafre in El Giza in Egypt. Donnelly used the fact that peoples in the Old and the New World had built pyramids as a cornerstone in his attempt to prove the existence of Atlantis. Right: the Castillo or Pyramid of Kukulcán at Chichén Itzá in Mexico. The Castillo was built some 4000 years after the Great Pyramids of Egypt, but it exhibits the same classic pyramid shape. Donnelly did not believe that it was possible for peoples working thousands of miles apart to have arrived independently at the same architectural forms. If "the great inventions were duplicated spontaneously," he wrote, "all savages would have invented the boomerang; all . . . would possess pottery, bows and arrows . . . and canoes. . . ."

Above: Donnelly used these drawings of a section of the treasure-house of Atreus at Mycenae in Greece (left) and the Arch of Las Monjas at Palenque in Central America (right) in his book *Atlantis* to illustrate the resemblance between the form of arch used in the oldest Greek buildings and that employed by American civilizations.

of years, thus indicating that it was imported from elsewhere. He quoted the opinion of the 19th-century French writer Ernest Renan to support this view: "Egypt at the beginning appears mature, old, and entirely without mythical and heroic ages, as if the country had never known youth. Its civilization has no infancy, and its art no archaic period." That opinion, together with "evidence" drawn from the religious and cultural beliefs of the ancient Egyptians and from their magnificent achievements, was sufficient to convince Donnelly that Egypt was colonized by survivors of Atlantis who brought with them a ready-made civilization modeled on their former life.

In Donnelly's view, the Mayas of Central America were also of Atlantean origin, partly because they possessed what he believed to be a phonetic alphabet similar to the Old World alphabets, and also because they "claim that their civilization came to them *across the sea in ships from the east,* that is, from the direction of Atlantis."

Another important feature of Donnelly's argument was the incidence of similar culture traits among New and Old World peoples, which he assumed to have a common origin. He cited as evidence the appearance on both sides of the Atlantic of pyramids, pillars, burial mounds, metallurgy, ships, and various other cultural developments. "I cannot believe that the great inventions were duplicated spontaneously . . . in different countries," he argued. "If this were so, all savages would have invented the boomerang; all savages would possess pottery, bow and arrows, slings, tents, and canoes; in short, all races would have risen to civilization, for certainly the comforts of life are as agreeable to one people as another."

Finally, this wide-ranging scholar claimed to have proved the connection between Atlantis and other civilizations through a study of linguistics. New World languages, he declared, are

Above: Egyptian bas-relief of the head of a young man, dating from about 1370 B.C. His forehead is flattened in a way characteristic of ancient Egyptian portrait heads. Right: mid-19th-century illustration of an American Indian woman and child of the Flat-Head tribe. The woman's forehead is flattened much like that of the Egyptian youth above. Donnelly took the existence of skull deformation in the Old and the New World, with the presence in both of similar architectural forms, as evidence that "the people of both . . . were originally united in blood and race"—the race of Atlantis.

closely related to tongues of the Old World, and he composed parallel tables of words to back his case. For those who had wanted to believe in Atlantis but had felt Plato's account left too many questions unanswered, Donnelly had put flesh on the bones of the legend. Almost every writer on Atlantis who came after him has borrowed from Donnelly's work, which remains the bible of Atlantology. But does it deserve that reputation?

Donnelly's forceful style, his undoubted learning, his enthusiasm, and his air of absolute conviction tend to sweep the reader along with him and mask the false or shaky foundations of some of his arguments. According to L. Sprague de Camp, author of one of the best critical studies of Atlantis, *Lost Continents*, "Most of Donnelly's statements of fact, to tell the truth, either were wrong when he made them, or have been disproved by subsequent discoveries."

De Camp points out that Donnelly was mistaken in asserting that the Peruvian Indians had a system of writing, or that the cotton plants native to the New and Old Worlds belong to the same species. Donnelly's comparisons between New and Old World alphabets were based on an inaccurate and discredited representation of a so-called "Mayan alphabet," further dis-

Above right: poster advertising a lecture given by Donnelly in 1889. His long hours of study in the Library of Congress and at his Nininger home were rewarded during his lecture tours when he spoke on such subjects as Wit and Humor—far removed from his main interests, politics and archaeology.

Right: cartoon of British statesman W. E. Gladstone published in 1869 in the journal *Vanity Fair*. Gladstone was so impressed by the evidence Donnelly had amassed to prove the existence of Atlantis that he tried—unsuccessfully—to obtain funds for a British expedition to search for the continent. Like many others, he failed to see the misconceptions and inaccuracies that Donnelly's argument contains.

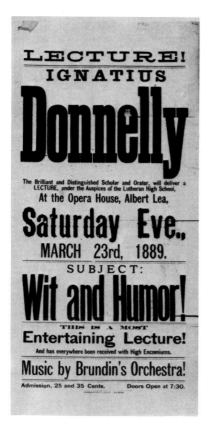

torted by Donnelly to create "intermediate forms" between Latin and allegedly Mayan letters. Nor is there a resemblance between the Otomi language of Mexico and Chinese, despite a table of "similarities" that Donnelly published. "I don't know what he used for Chinese," says de Camp, "—certainly not the standard Northern Chinese, the language usually meant by the term."

Errors such as these have gone largely unnoticed, and Donnelly still enjoys a sizable following. Soon after the publication of his first book his correspondence reached gigantic proportions. Even the British Prime Minister William E. Gladstone is said to have written to express his appreciation. Gladstone was so impressed by Donnelly's arguments that he tried to persuade Parliament to vote funds for an expedition to go in search of Atlantis. On the strength of such reactions, Donnelly took to the lecture platform with equal success. Then he turned his back on lecturing to return home and continue writing. Later, he re-entered politics, helping to found the Populist Party, and twice running for Vice-President of the United States on the Populist ticket. This remarkable, largely self-taught man died in 1901, knowing that he had shaped and laid the foundation stone of modern Atlantology.

Others soon followed, of whom the most outstanding was Lewis Spence, a Scottish mythologist who launched a short-lived magazine called *Atlantis Quarterly* and wrote five books on Atlantis. Spence never achieved the popular appeal of Donnelly, but his theories have won almost as much acclaim among fellow Atlantologists. Even the skeptics have a high regard for Spence. L. Sprague de Camp, for instance, calls Spence "a sane and sober writer," and describes his major work, *The Problem of Atlantis*, as "about the best pro-Atlantis work published to date."

Like Donnelly, Spence takes a serious and scientific approach to his subject. In *The Problem of Atlantis*, which appeared in 1924, he set out to prove four points:

"1. That a great continent formerly occupied the whole or major portion of the North Atlantic region, and a considerable portion of its southern basin. Of early geological origin, it must, in the course of successive ages, have experienced many changes in contour and mass, probably undergoing frequent submergence and emergence.

"2. That in the Miocene (Later Tertiary) times [from 25 to 10 million years ago] it still retained its continental character, but towards the end of that period it began to disintegrate, owing to successive volcanic and other causes.

"3. That this disintegration resulted in the formation of greater and lesser insular masses. Two of these, considerably larger in area than any of the others, were situated (a) at a relatively short distance from the entrance to the Mediterranean; and (b) in the region of the present West Indian Islands. These may respectively be called Atlantis and Antillia. Communication between them was possible by an insular chain.

"4. That these two island-continents and this connecting chain of islands persisted until late Pleistocene times, at which epoch (about 25,000 years ago, or the beginning of the post-glacial epoch) Atlantis seems to have experienced further disintegration.

Above: Scottish Atlantist Lewis Spence. Like Donnelly, Spence approached his subject scientifically, attempting to produce evidence in support of his four theses about Atlantis. Unlike Donnelly's theories, however, Spence's theses were principally concerned with the geographical existence and disappearance of the lost continent, rather than with the Atlantean civilization and its effects.

Final disaster appears to have overtaken Atlantis about 10,000 B.C. Antillia, on the other hand, seems to have survived until a much more recent period, and still persists fragmentally in the Antillean group, or West Indian Islands."

In order to make these theses acceptable, Spence had to throw out some aspects of Plato's account. Atlantis, he asserted, did not vanish in a day and a night. Its disappearance—the last of many disasters affecting the continent—probably occurred gradually over many years. Nor did he attempt to confirm Donnelly's claim that Atlantis was the source of all civilization. Although he believed the Atlanteans had a developed culture, he was prepared to accept that they were a Stone Age people, despite Plato's reference to their skillful use of metals.

If Atlantis did exist in the Atlantic Ocean, Spence argued, and disintegrated gradually—finally disappearing at about the time Plato gives (around 10,000 B.C.)—then there should be evidence of its survivors taking refuge in other lands. In the early phases of Atlantis's destruction, man was not a seafarer, and the Atlantean landmass must have been near the coast of other continents to make the journey possible. Spence is able to produce some fascinating evidence for just such an exodus.

The missing link between the Atlanteans and present-day man, according to Spence, consisted of three races of people, the Cro-Magnon, the Caspian, and the Azilian. Quoting a variety of experts Spence demonstrates that none of these races developed in the country where their remains are now to be found. Because most of their settlements were in the coastal areas of southwestern France and northern Spain, around the shores of the Bay of Biscay, Spence concluded that they came from a country to the west. None exists there now, and it must have been Atlantis.

The Cro-Magnons were the first to arrive in Europe, at the close of the Ice Age about 25,000 years ago. They appear to have wiped out the Neanderthal people who then inhabited the area, which is hardly surprising because the Cro-Magnons were vastly superior in physique and intellect. The average height of the Cro-Magnon men was 6 feet $1\frac{1}{2}$ inches. They had short arms—a sign of high racial development—and skulls that indicate an exceptionally large brain capacity. Their faces were very broad, with massive chins, high foreheads, and beak noses. The Cro-Magnon people produced amazingly realistic cave paintings—usually of animals, including the bull—and carved equally impressive pictures on their tools and utensils.

This remarkable race flourished for 15,000 years until it was displaced by the Caspian and Azilian invasions. According to Spence, these peoples were also fleeing from Atlantis at later periods in the island's violent history. The Azilians appeared in exactly the same European areas as their predecessors, but archaeologists have found evidence that, unlike the Cro-Magnon people, the Azilians were fishermen, capable of deep-sea fishing. If subsequent cataclysms had destroyed the land-bridge that brought the Cro-Magnons to Europe, said Spence, their successors now had boats in which to flee. Azilian culture appeared in Europe around 10,000 B.C., which ties in approximately with Plato's date for the destruction of Atlantis. Significantly, the

Above: Spence's map of Atlantis (A) and Antillia (B). Spence believed that Atlantis broke up over a considerable period of time, rather than disappearing overnight as Plato described. The first stage in the disintegration was its break-up into two smaller landmasses, Atlantis and Antillia. According to Spence, Atlantis later disappeared, but fragments of Antillia still exist—the Antilles or West Indies. Right: artist's impression of Cro-Magnon man, who flourished in Europe from about 25,000 years ago. Spence believed that the Cro-Magnon people came originally from Atlantis, and he produced an impressive array of evidence to support his claim. As Atlantis disintegrated, Spence asserted, further waves of survivors fled east to Europe. The Cro-Magnons were followed first by the Caspians, then by the Azilian race.

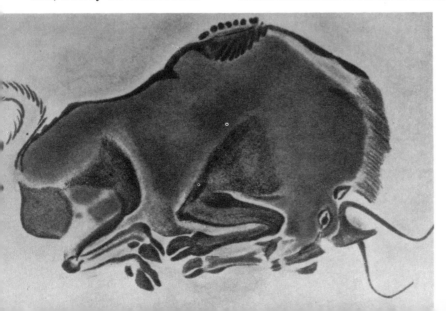

Left: Cro-Magnon painting of a charging bison, from the roof of a cave at Altamira, Spain. Spence, identifying the bison with the bull, cites these paintings as evidence of Cro-Magnon man's Atlantean origin. The bull, Plato records, had been especially reverenced by the Atlantean race.

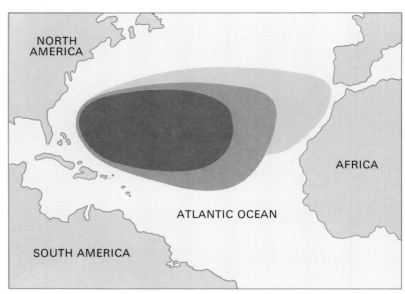

NORTH AMERICA

AFRICA

ATLANTIC OCEAN

SOUTH AMERICA

Azilians were always buried facing west—toward their homeland, according to Spence.

Spence argued that the Azilians probably founded the civilizations of Egypt and Crete. He believed that Atlantean town planning, as described by Plato, was reflected in the great ancient cities of Carthage and Knossos. In Spence's view, the Mayan culture too derived from Atlantis—as Donnelly had claimed before him. He explained the enormous time gap between the destruction of Atlantis around 10,000 B.C. and the appearance of the Mayan civilization just before the Christian Era by suggesting that some Atlantean refugees had fled westward to Antillia (the second island continent in his theory) and had remained there for thousands of years. It was only when Antillia too was destroyed that they moved on to Central America. Spence believed that the Mayan culture, like that of Egypt, was imported, because it showed no evidence of gradual evolution.

Mankind may have largely forgotten Atlantis over the centuries, argued Spence, but certain animals did not. As an example, he pointed to the curious behavior of the Norwegian lemming. When the lemming population outgrows its local food supply, these small rodents gather in great masses and swim out to sea until they all drown. In Spence's view the lemmings are responding to an instinctive memory of a land that used to exist in the west, where fresh food could be found.

Despite his praise of Spence's book, L. Sprague de Camp is quickly on hand to raise a few healthy objections to some of the author's conclusions. "Even if we confine ourselves to Spence's facts, they turn out less impressive than they seem at first," he writes. "For one thing, Cro-Magnon culture has now been found in the East—in Palestine. Furthermore, despite all these assertions that the cultures of Egypt, Yucatán, and Peru sprang into existence suddenly without a slow transition from primitive culture, modern archaeology has disclosed the gradual evolution of all these cultures from more primitive levels. You can, for instance, trace the growth of Egyptian culture from the neolithic Merimda people, who wore animal skins, lived in mud houses, and farmed in a crude manner, to the highly civilized men of the Fourth Dynasty."

It is easy enough to make mistakes about the development of cultures, says de Camp, simply because relics of more recent times are more numerous and easier to find, and are frequently bigger and more durable than those built in a culture's earlier stages. In Spence's defense, however, modern Atlantologists point to numerous relics and artifacts that do not appear to fit in with the archaeologists' neat and orderly pattern of development.

As for the lemmings in search of a lost land, de Camp points out that when they become starved by overpopulation they set off willy-nilly in any direction, often swimming rivers in search of food. When they reach the sea they no doubt mistake it for another river and carry on swimming until they drown. Swedish lemmings, he adds, try to swim the Baltic in the opposite direction, which makes nonsense of Spence's theory . . . unless, of course, Atlantis was in the Baltic, as one researcher has suggested.

Lewis Spence, who died in 1955, would probably not have been

Left: miniature illustrating a manuscript of the voyages of St. Brendan, Abbot of Clauinfert, Ireland, in the 6th century A.D. Accompanied by his monks, he set sail into the Atlantic in search of a land where he would find converts to Christianity, and according to the account of his voyage he was successful in the search. In the minds of Atlantists, such medieval accounts of new lands in the Atlantic Ocean became identified with the Atlantis myth.

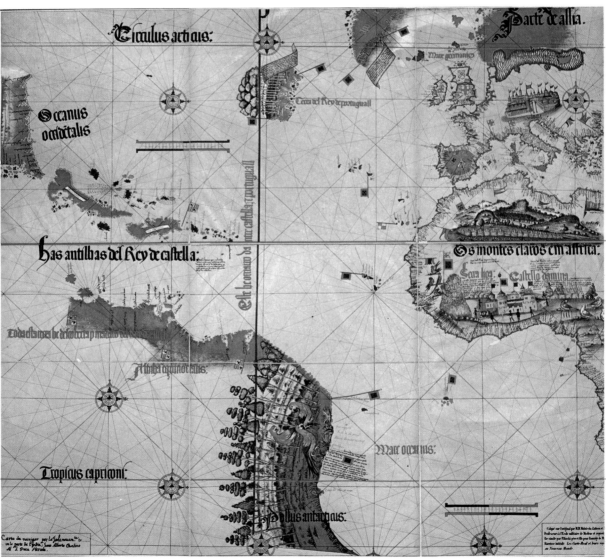

too perturbed by such criticisms. Although he had worked hard to assemble facts on which to hang his theories, he realized that ultimately they would probably not be sufficient to convince the skeptics. His books do not openly deal with the occult aspects of Atlantology, but Spence was certainly aware that many had endeavored to solve the riddle of the lost continent by non-material methods. Indeed, before writing his first book on Atlantis, Spence had completed an excellent *Encyclopedia of Occultism*, in which he made a first cautious reference to Atlantis.

In time, Spence grew tired of the demand for facts. He began suggesting that the durability of the Atlantis theory might be due to a common "folk-memory" that could actually be inherited rather than preserved through oral or written accounts. There is "a world-intuition regarding the existence of a transatlantic continent," he said, and "we are dealing with a great world-memory, of which Plato's story is merely one of the broken and distorted fragments. . . ." Elsewhere he declared himself in favor of "inspirational methods," which would become "the Archaeology of the Future." In his opinion, "The Tape-Measure School, dull and full of the credulity of incredulity, is doomed," and "the day is passing when mere weight of evidence alone, unsupported by considerations which result from inspiration or insight, can be accepted by the world."

Many Atlantis enthusiasts have been satisfied with inspiration alone, of course, but Spence's views rather clouded his reputation as a scholar. Spence did little to allay his critics when, in 1942, he published a book entitled *Will Europe Follow Atlantis?* This argued that God had destroyed Atlantis because of the wickedness of the Atlanteans and (with the Nazi atrocities in mind) He would do the same to Europe unless it reformed.

For all his idiosyncrasies Spence is probably still the best guide to the Atlantis story. His knowledge of the subject was such that he was consulted by Sir Arthur Conan Doyle during the latter's preparation of his exciting romance *The Lost World*, which concerns an expedition to the Brazilian jungle in search of a mysterious, hidden world. Spence also conducted a correspondence with an English explorer, Colonel Percy H. Fawcett, who was planning a very similar expedition. Fawcett believed that South America might be part of Atlantis, or that the mysterious cities reported to exist in the dense jungles of the Amazon might have been built by Atlanteans who had fled their stricken land.

Fawcett was not alone in linking ancient America with Atlantis. Both Donnelly and Spence had used the Mayan culture as evidence in their arguments, and the mysterious early civilizations of the Americas still fascinate and puzzle us today.

Above: Spence used this stone figure found in a grave in Mexico as the frontispiece to his *History of Atlantis*. According to his theory, it represents one of the soldiers of Atlantis wearing Atlantean armor of the Mexican type.

3

The Ancient Legacy

High on a desolate plateau in the Andes stand the ruins of an ancient city, silent, shadowy, and mysterious. This is Tiahuanaco, near La Paz in modern Bolivia. Set at the dizzying altitude of 13,000 feet, amid a wild expanse of barren rock, framed by volcanic mountains, Tiahuanaco is one of the loneliest and most inhospitable places on earth. Yet this city was once the heart of a mighty civilization, built by an unknown people who lived on the shores of Lake Titicaca hundreds—and perhaps many thousands—of years before the arrival of the Incas. Legend has it that Tiahuanaco was built for the worship of Viracocha, the

Above: turquoise mosaic mask of Quetzalcoatl, the Aztec god of learning. Aztec legend described Quetzalcoatl as a fair-skinned god who had brought civilization to Mexico from across the sea. Similar White Gods appear in mythologies of the Incas and the Mayas too— the Incas called him Viracocha, the Mayas Kukulcán. Many believe that these White Gods must be based on a common racial memory of fair-skinned visitors from other lands.

Right: idol and altar at Copan, Honduras, drawn by British explorer Frederick Catherwood. In the 1840s Catherwood and American traveler John Stephens discovered relics of pre-Columbian American civilizations. Their discoveries caused a considerable stir. How, the world asked, could the peoples of America have built such edifices alone?

44

"The most impressive feature...is the Gate of the Sun"

White God, who came to the Indians in the distant past, bringing them all the arts and laws of an advanced civilization. Then Viracocha disappeared across the sea, never fulfilling his promise to return.

Tiahuanaco already lay partly in ruins when the Incas found it in the early 13th century A.D. Three hundred years later the Spanish conquistadors destroyed more of the city in their search for gold. The destruction of Tiahuanaco continued at the end of the 19th century, when most of its remaining treasures were plundered; its fabulous buildings and massive statues were blasted away to provide building materials for the city of La Paz and a roadbed for its railroad. However, enough was recorded by Spanish chroniclers and by travelers from later times for us to be able to gain some impression of the former majesty of this great city and of the powerful and gifted people who built it.

Tiahuanaco now stands about 15 miles from Lake Titicaca, but the level of the lake has dropped considerably over the centuries and its waters once lapped the very walls of the ancient city. Stairs led from the water up the side of a massive step pyramid, about 150 feet tall, topped by a huge temple. Palaces, temples, and other great buildings stood on the shores of the lake. One Spanish chronicler, Diego d'Alcobaca, reported seeing a paved court 80 feet square, with a covered hall 45 feet long running down one of its sides. The court and hall had been hewn from a single block of stone. "There are still many statues to be seen here today," wrote d'Alcobaca. "They represent men and women, and are so perfect one could believe the figures were alive." Another chronicler held that, "One of the palaces is truly an eighth wonder of the world. Stones 37 feet long by 15 feet wide have been prepared without the aid of lime or mortar, in such a way as to fit together without any joins showing." The Spanish discovered that the colossal stone blocks—some of them weighing as much as 200 tons—used in these buildings were held in place by silver rivets. (It was the removal of these rivets by Spanish mercenaries that caused many of Tiahuanaco's great buildings to collapse in subsequent earthquakes.) The blocks were brought from the volcanic Kiappa region, 40 miles from Tiahuanaco, and, as writer and South American explorer Pierre Honoré comments in his book *In Quest of the White God*, "As with the pyramids in Egypt, thousands of men must have worked for hundreds of years to erect the enormous buildings of Tiahuanaco, slave labor forced to build on an ever larger, taller, more powerful scale."

The most impressive feature of Tiahuanaco that is still standing is the Gate of the Sun, which may have been the entrance to the city or to its main palace. Cut from a single block of stone, 10 feet high, 6 feet wide, and weighing over 10 tons, it is the largest carved monolith on earth. The gate is crowned by a deeply carved frieze of beautiful and intricate designs, including human figures, animals, birds, and symbols thought by some investigators to denote astronomical observations. Over the center of the gate is a stylized jaguar with human features, holding what may be symbols of thunder and lightning. The frieze was originally inlaid with gold, and the eyes of the figures were made of semi-precious stones. Some of the carvings have been left unfinished,

Left: stone figure from the ancient city of Tiahuanaco in what is now Bolivia. The city was discovered by the Incas in the 13th century A.D., later pillaged by the Spanish conquistadors, and largely destroyed in the 19th century to provide building stone. Even from what remains, however, we can glimpse the splendor it once enjoyed. Tradition has it that this magnificent city was built for the worship of the White God Viracocha, and was once inhabited by the Incas. But exactly when it was constructed, and by whom, remains a mystery still.

Right: the Gate of the Sun at Tiahuanaco. Once the entrance to a temple or a palace, perhaps, this gateway is surmounted by an intricately carved frieze depicting people, animals, birds, and enigmatic symbols or signs. When the city was at its prime, the frieze was inlaid with gold and semiprecious stones, but—like so many of the other valuable relics of American civilizations—these have long disappeared, plundered by travelers greedy for wealth.

Above: Mayan temple at Tuloom in Central America, found by Stephens and Catherwood and drawn by Catherwood. In describing this temple the explorers mentioned that it was so overgrown with creepers and trees that they had found it purely by chance. It was due to the luxuriant growth of the Central and South American jungles that the relics of America's pro-Columbian civilizations remained hidden for so many years.

as if something had suddenly interrupted the work of the artists.

According to Spanish chroniclers, the walls and niches of Tiahuanaco's palaces and temples were adorned with statues and ornaments of gold, copper, and bronze, and with stone and clay masks that hung from large-headed gold nails. The holes made by these nails can still be seen today, and some of the nails and other precious objects salvaged from the ruins of Tiahuanaco are on view in La Paz in the Posnansky Museum—named for Arthur Posnansky, a German engineer who tried to save Tiahuanaco from further destruction during the quarrying operations of the 19th century. Pieces in the museum and in private collections include six-foot-high statues covered all over with reliefs, gold figurines weighing between four and six pounds, gold animals and birds, and gold cups, plates, and spoons. These few remaining treasures testify to Tiahuanaco's former magnificence, and other groups of ruins, including step pyramids, in the highlands and on the coast of present-day Bolivia and Peru indicate the power and extent of the ancient Tiahuanacan civilization.

Tiahuanaco has puzzled archaeologists and historians ever since its discovery. Although our knowledge of the history and development of the civilization of South and Central America has increased enormously in recent years, and the experts have

been able to answer some questions about the majestic city, the riddle of its age and of the people who built it is by no means solved.

When archaeologists and explorers of the 19th and early 20th century began rediscovering the magnificent stone citadels of once flourishing civilizations in Central and South America, the effect was electrifying. Most Europeans and North Americans, accustomed to regarding the Middle East as the cradle of civilization, found it hard to believe that the American Indians could possibly have developed such a high degree of cultural and technical achievement without outside help. In the 1840s, when the American traveler John Lloyd Stephens first uncovered the awesome vestiges of Mayan civilization deep in the Honduran jungle, he declared himself convinced that the local inhabitants could not have built such structures. Whenever the remains of advanced civilizations were found in the Americas, they were attributed to the influence of Old World peoples such as the Egyptians, the Phoenicians, the Irish, or the Vikings—or to the Atlanteans. Atlantists were quick to seize on the discovery of American pre-Columbian civilizations as further evidence for the existence of a lost Atlantic continent. After all, Plato had mentioned another great continent that lay beyond Atlantis on the other side of the ocean, and had said that Atlantean influence

Above: huge stone head sculpted by the Olmecs, founders of the earliest known American civilization. To a world that had regarded the Middle East as the cradle of civilization, the discovery of a culturally advanced people in the Americas was an amazing one. Below: 16th-century Peruvian gold statuette of a toucan. The Incas of Peru brought the art of gold-working to seldom equaled heights.

49

Left: Olmec pottery statuette. No one knows where the Olmecs came from, but their civilization flourished around the Gulf of Mexico between about 1300 and 400 B.C.

Right: an Aztec scouting expedition and punitive raid, from the *Codex Mendoza*. The Aztecs were a warlike and bloodthirsty people, who spread their rule over a large part of Central America between about A.D. 1350 and their conquest by the Spanish in 1521. The *Codex Mendoza* records the life and history of Mexico under Aztec rule. It was commissioned after the conquest of Mexico by the Spanish governor-general.

extended to parts of that continent. Direct contact between the Old World and the New prior to the arrival of Columbus in 1492 must have been chancy and sporadic, if it occurred at all, the Atlantists argued, simply because of the vast expanses of ocean that lie between the two. But if the Atlanteans were even half as powerful as Plato had described them, a voyage from their Atlantic home to the Americas would have been easy, especially considering the chain of islands that were said to stretch across the ocean between Atlantis and the outer continent.

Did the Atlanteans influence the civilizations of Central and South America? It is a possibility that has to be considered in any attempt to unravel the mysteries of the ancient ruins in this part of the world. If we reject the theory, we are still faced with the questions: Who built these fabulous cities? And how did they acquire the technical skills to do so?

In trying to answer these questions we have to take into account the theory of cultural diffusion. This is based on the belief that separate civilizations would not develop along similar lines without contact with each other. Where we find two or more cultures with the same or similar beliefs, customs, art forms, architecture, or technologies, we can assume, according to the theory, that the people concerned acquired their knowledge from each other, or from a common source. This was the cornerstone of Ignatius Donnelly's arguments about Atlantis, and although there are many diffusionists who do not believe in Atlantis, almost all latter-day Atlantists believe in diffusion because it fits their case so well. It is because of some remarkable cultural similarities that the civilizations of the Americas share among themselves and with those of the Old World that most believers in Atlantis look upon the now ruined citadels of Central and South America as outposts of the once great Atlantean culture.

Orthodox scholars challenge this view. Today many scholars believe that the pre-Columbian civilizations of the Americas were developed by the American Indians themselves, independent of any chance contact they may have had with the outside world. The only trouble from the scholars' point of view is that they have so far been unable to trace with any certainty the starting point of civilization in the Americas. No sooner do they uncover the origins of one civilization in this part of the world than another equally advanced civilization appears right behind it. This, of course, comes as no surprise to Atlantologists, who are convinced that a fully developed civilization was imported into the Americas in the first place.

Before examining this claim in detail, we need to take a look at what archaeologists know of the people in whose lands the mysterious citadels of the Americas have appeared. They are principally the Olmecs, the Mayas, the Incas, and the Aztecs. The Olmec civilization is the oldest so far known in the Americas, and was founded along the Gulf of Mexico in what are now the states of Veracruz and Tabasco. No one knows where the Olmecs came from, but their civilization is thought to have flourished from about 1300 B.C. to 400 B.C., and their colossal monuments and sculptures show them to have been gifted artists and engineers. They also possessed a written language, apparently resembling that of the Mayas, whose origins are equally mysterious. The Mayan culture arose in Guatemala some time between 400 and 100 B.C. and flourished there for 1000 years, during which the Mayas built over 100 city-states with magnificent temples, palaces, pyramids, and plazas. The Mayas called themselves "lords of the earth," and their influence quickly spread toward the north, west, and southwest, covering a large part of Central America. Then, between A.D. 700 and 1000, for reasons that are still unknown, they abandoned their homeland and its thriving cities and moved to the arid and inhospitable Yucatán.

Left: the Emperor Atahualpa, ruler of the Incas when the Spanish conquistadors arrived in Peru. When his empire fell to the Spanish in 1537, Inca civilization had existed little more than 300 years, yet in that time Inca rule had spread across a vast area. Right: Mayan relief of woman ceremonially mutilating her tongue. Mayan culture flourished in Central America for about 1000 years.

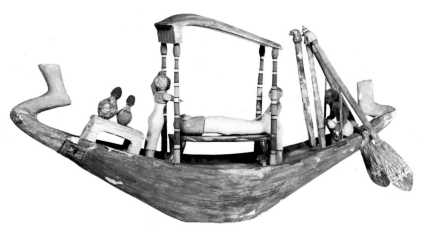

Above: model of a papyrus boat, found in an ancient Egyptian tomb.
Right: reed boats on the waters of Lake Titicaca in Bolivia. These
vessels are similar to those of ancient Egypt in shape, materials,
and construction. According to the theory of cultural diffusion,
such similarity would be impossible unless the civilizations had
had contact, or had acquired their knowledge from a common source.
Atlantists believe this source to be the lost continent of Atlantis.
Below: Norwegian anthropologist Thor Heyerdahl's reed boat *Ra II*.
Heyerdahl attempted an Atlantic crossing in *Ra II* to prove that the
ancient Egyptians could have brought civilization to the Americas.

Their attempts to rebuild their empire were thwarted by invasions and internal strife, and the Mayan civilization gradually declined. By the time the Spaniards arrived in 1511 it possessed only a shadow of its former greatness.

The Aztecs of Mexico were relative latecomers on the American scene. Their civilization flourished from about 1350 until the Spanish conquest of 1521. They inherited much of their culture from their predecessors, but their own art and architecture was so splendid that the leader of the Spanish conquistadors declared their capital Tenochtitlán (now the site of Mexico City): "The most beautiful city in the world." While the Aztecs were building Tenochtitlán, the Incas of South America were establishing their considerable empire that stretched from the Columbia-Ecuador border to central Chile, taking in parts of present-day Peru, northern Argentina, Bolivia, Chile, and Ecuador. The Incas, who founded their capital of Cusco around A.D. 1200 and whose empire crumbled before the Spaniards in 1537, traced their ancestry back in legend to the builders of Tiahuanaco, which they regarded as the cradle of their civilization.

The history books, then, paint a picture of a whole series of rapidly developing American civilizations, far less ancient than those of the Old World, and archaeological examination of the ruins generally confirms this simplified view of the various peoples of the Americas. But some scholars disagree. Tiahuanaco, for example, has been the center of debate for decades because the experts cannot agree about when the city was built. At one time it was widely believed to date from around 1000 B.C. Today, the generally accepted view is that its impressive buildings were erected several centuries after the beginning of our era—estimates vary from about A.D. 100 to 800. Some scholars believe several cities were built on the same site. Arthur Posnansky, who made valiant efforts to preserve the ruins of Tiahuanaco, came to the conclusion that the last city was built 16,000 years ago. Other researchers claim that Tiahuanaco is a quarter of a million years old.

It has been suggested that Tiahuanaco was originally built at sea level and that the land on which it now stands and Lake Titicaca were thrust upward a distance of about two miles during a convulsion of the earth many thousands of years ago. This theory is based on the discovery of a "water mark" line on the surrounding mountains, which stretches for over 300 miles and consists of the calcified remains of marine plants, indicating that these slopes were once part of the seashore. Significantly Lake Titicaca has a very high salinity and oceanic fauna, as do other lakes in the area. This theory would certainly account for the presence of what appears to be a ruined seaport close to Tiahuanaco and might also explain why the city was abruptly abandoned by its builders and how it first fell into ruin.

According to some German and local archaeologists, Tiahuanaco was abandoned around 9000 or 10,000 B.C.—which conveniently coincides with the date given by Plato for the destruction of Atlantis. Atlantologists conclude that the catastrophe that caused Atlantis to sink into the ocean also pushed a large area of the west coast of South America some two miles above sea level. If this theory were proved correct and

Tiahuanaco was built before the catastrophe, it would be over 11,000 years old.

Another curious feature of the area has not escaped the cultural diffusionists and the Atlantologists. The boats that sail on the salty waters of Lake Titicaca are identical with the papyrus boats of ancient Egypt. Their shape, the material used, and the method of construction are the same. Coincidence? Evidence of direct contact between ancient Egypt and the New World? Or one more clue that a long-lost civilization once influenced great areas of the globe?

South America is probably one of the last places on earth to be keeping its secrets from us. Many lost cities have been found in the dense, almost impenetrable jungle since the turn of the century, and no one can guess how many more, filled with treasures and works of art, are hidden beneath the thick and tangled canopy of tropical vegetation. It is an area that cannot easily be mapped from the air, and explorers enter this "Green Hell" at their peril.

Among the adventurers who have dared to risk death in their search for ancient ruins, the name of Colonel Percy H. Fawcett is particularly remembered because of the mystery surrounding the fate of his final expedition to South America. Fawcett was convinced that the ruins of Atlantis or some of its daughter cities lay beneath the jungles of Brazil, and in the 1920s, after 20 years in the British Army as a military surveyor, geographer, and engineer, he turned to exploration. He went on several expeditions to Brazil, during which he traveled extensively through uncharted country populated by hostile tribes. Fawcett was an acknowledged expert on the area and how to survive its hazards.

During these explorations a map came into his possession. It was said to have been 150 years old and to have been drawn by a man who had found a lost city deep in the Mato Grosso region of southwest Brazil. The city was said to be surrounded by a wall and to stand in acres of cultivated land. In 1925, accompanied by his 20-year-old son Jack and a young friend named Raleigh Rimmel, Fawcett set off in search of this city, which he was sure would prove to have links with Atlantis. Before his departure, he declared: "Whether we succeed in penetrating the jungle and come out alive, or whether we leave our bones there, of this I am certain: the key to the mystery of ancient South America, and perhaps of the whole of prehistory, can be found if we are able to locate these old cities . . . and open them up to science. Their existence I do not for a moment doubt—how could I? I myself have seen a portion of one, and that is the reason why I observed it was imperative for me to go again. The remains seemed to be those of an outpost of one of the largest cities, which I am convinced is to be found together with others, if a properly organized search is carried out. Unfortunately I cannot induce scientific men to accept even the supposition that there are traces of an old civilization in Brazil. But I have traveled through regions unknown to other explorers and the wild Indians have told me time and again of the buildings, the characteristics of their old inhabitants, and the strange things to be found there."

With those words, Fawcett and his two companions left for their last great adventure. Their final message came from Dead

Above: Percy Harrison Fawcett, leader of one of the most famous expeditions ever to set out in search of a lost land. While traveling in South America, Fawcett came into possession of a map showing the location of a lost city that he called "X." In 1925, Fawcett set out in search of X with his son Jack and a friend but no member of their party was ever seen again.

Horse Camp in the Xingú Basin, where they reported hearing of yet another ruined city on the edge of a large lake. Then they disappeared into the jungle, never to be seen again. The chances are that they were captured and killed by hostile Indians or that they all died from fever. But as the world waited for news of the Fawcett expedition, other theories were advanced. Some believed that the party had found the lost city but, for reasons best known to themselves, had decided not to return to England. Others suggested that the Indians had taken the explorers to the lost city but had either killed them or held them prisoner afterward so that no one else would come looking for the secret.

Above: Jack Fawcett and Raleigh Rimmel at Dead Horse Camp during the expedition in search of X. The last message ever to be received from the party came from Dead Horse Camp—in it, Fawcett wrote that he had heard of another ruined city beside a large lake. The world waited in suspense to hear whether or not Fawcett had found the city but no further news of the party ever appeared.

Left: drawing by Brian Fawcett of his father's expedition encountering Amazonian Indians. When the Fawcett party failed to reappear from the jungle, one explanation put forward was that they had been killed or permanently imprisoned by Indians. Others believed that they had found the city for which they were searching and had decided never to return.

Mediums tried to contact Fawcett in the next world, but their psychic explorations shed little light on the true outcome of his expedition.

Nevertheless, one alleged spirit communication does stand head and shoulders above the others. This purports to be a long communication from Fawcett, dictated over a number of years through the hand of a woman who was to become one of the world's most famous automatic writing mediums.

Geraldine Cummins, a young Irish writer, was already a well-known medium when her friend, E. Beatrice Gibbes, asked her to try communicating with the lost explorer. Miss Cummins would go into a light trance during which her hand would be allegedly controlled by spirit people who would write messages. It was 10 years after Fawcett had disappeared when the two women first attempted to establish contact with him. They apparently succeeded, but Fawcett told them he was not dead. He was in a semi-conscious state, still in the South American jungle, but his spirit was able to communicate. Four communications were made in 1936, after which they were abandoned for 13 years. When Fawcett again communicated, in 1948, he said he had died.

It would be easy to dismiss these messages as utter nonsense if it were not for the fact that Geraldine Cummins was a very talented psychic widely respected in psychical research. She submitted to numerous tests during her long lifetime, and was apparently able to receive communications of incredible detail and accuracy from people about whom she knew nothing. Researchers are still debating whether in the best of these cases Geraldine Cummins was really in touch with the dead person, or whether she was using clairvoyance to discover information that she could not know normally. There is no doubt, however, that she did possess remarkable paranormal powers. So, even if she was not in touch with Fawcett, the possibility exists that she did have supernormal access to facts about the fate and findings of his expedition.

The communicator claiming to be Fawcett wrote that he had seen pyramids in the jungle. He had apparently been given drugs that enabled him, when in the vicinity of a certain pyramid, to travel back in time. The forest would become transparent and another landscape would appear before his eyes, superimposed on the jungle. He could then see the pyramids as they had been in the distant past and the people who lived at that time. He described the pyramids as Egyptian in appearance.

"You must accept my assurance that the last relics of an ancient civilization, Egyptian in character, are to be found in central South America," he wrote. "With my living eyes I have seen these ruins. . . . I believe that, if the climate were not so oppressive and we could bring gangs of men here, excavating under skilled direction, a whole ancient civilization would be revealed—the secret of the Lost Continent would be divulged; a flood of light thrown on a period that is prehistoric, and our origins more clearly realized."

The communicator said that sun worship was the basic principle of this civilization, and he added: "The Atlanteans knew more or less the nature of electricity, which is dependent on the sun yet is allied to other air forces. Of course, there is more

Above: in 1951, 26 years after Fawcett's disappearance, these bones were found in a shallow grave in the jungle. Exhibited in Rio de Janeiro as Fawcett's, they were later proved not to be his. Below: the jungle grave in which bones said to be those of Fawcett were found in 1951. This photograph was taken by Brian Fawcett.

than one kind of electricity. The kind that is known to men was discovered by these Atlanteans, but they used their kind of electricity in a different way from us. They realized that it might be used, not merely to give light—queer globular lights—but that it might also be employed in connection with the shifting of weights. The building of the pyramids is solved when you know that huge blocks of stone can be manipulated through what I might call blast-electricity. . . . You will think me mad . . . but I, who have seen this ancient world, walked through its streets, halted before the porticoes of its temples, descended into the great subterranean world wherein electricity and air are combined and fused, can assure you that the men who came before modern history was recorded knew more about matter and light, about the ether and its properties, than the scientists of the 20th century can ever know or imagine."

The scripts went on to claim that it was not natural forces but massive explosions in these subterranean electricity reservoirs that destroyed Atlantis. Do these writings give us a fantastic glimpse of Atlantis, or are they simply the outpourings of a highly imaginative brain? It is not a question we can answer with certainty. There is undoubtedly a widespread belief that ancient peoples were able to move great weights by unknown means, though scholars have come back with quite mundane solutions to such problems. The ancient Egyptian pyramids have often been cited in this connection despite the experts' assurances that thousands of labourers *were* capable of moving and assembling the huge blocks used in their construction.

In the Americas, too, we find immense buildings made of huge blocks of stone, often greater than those of the Egyptian pyramids. Time and again we learn that the stones were cut with such precision that the joins between them were scarcely detectable, and required no mortar. Yet the people who designed and built these architectural masterpieces possessed neither iron nor steel. Nor was bronze in general use, for either tools or weapons. Many temples, and even cities, were built high in the mountains, where the problems of terrain and altitude made their construction even more difficult.

Of all these cyclopean structures, the one that raises the biggest question mark over the Americas is undoubtedly the pyramid. Understandably, the sight of these impressive monuments calls to mind the Egyptians. Is it possible that two quite separate civilizations, living at different times, evolved the same structure and the technique to build it?

L. Sprague de Camp can be relied on to throw cold water on any Atlantis or other diffusionist theory not backed by scientific evidence. "Mayan architecture, like that of Egypt three or four thousand years earlier, began by developing stone structures in imitation of the existing wooden houses . . ." he writes in *Lost Continents*. "Their structures included astronomical observatories, ball-courts in which they played a kind of cross between basket-ball and soccer, dance-platforms, vapor-baths, shrines, reviewing-stands, stadiums, city walls, causeways, and pyramids, comparable in bulk, though not in height, with those of Egypt. However, the pyramids of the Mayas and Aztecs have nothing to do with those of Egypt, which were built several thousands of

years earlier and moreover evolved from tombs, while the New-World pyramids evolved from temple platforms.''

But for once, de Camp cannot have the last word. Despite his assertion that Egyptian and American pyramids differ in that the former evolved from tombs and the latter from temples, some New World pyramids were used for burial in a similar way to those in Egypt. And that, say the Atlantologists, is stretching coincidence too far.

It was in 1952, when Professor Alberto Ruz Lhullier was investigating the Mayan ruins near Palenque in southeast Mexico, that the burial aspect of American pyramids was confirmed. Among the ruins in Palenque is an impressive step pyramid known as the Temple of the Inscriptions. Inside this pyramid, Lhullier found a passage blocked with rubble. When this was removed and the professor had reached what he took to be the base of the pyramid, he discovered a heavy stone door. Behind it lay a chamber, 12 feet by 7 feet, whose floor consisted of a slab decorated with reliefs. Using an elaborate system of ropes and pulleys, Lhullier and his team finally managed to lift the 12-cwt slab. Beneath it they found a large, red stone sarcophagus containing the skeleton of a man, and a quantity of jade treasure, including a death mask placed over the man's skull. The walls of the tomb were covered with stucco relief figures of men in archaic costume—possibly ancestors of the Mayans who built the city near Palenque.

Commenting on this remarkable find, Michael Coe, Professor of Anthropology at Yale University, writes in his book *The Maya*: "It is immediately evident that this great man, certainly a late seventh- or early eighth-century ruler of Palenque, had the Funerary Crypt built to contain his own remains; further, that he might have had the entire temple pyramid above it raised in his own lifetime. Thus it seems that the Temple of the Inscriptions was a funerary monument with exactly the same primary function as the Egyptian pyramids. And this, of course, leads one to look upon most Maya temple pyramids as sepulchral monuments, dedicated to the worship of deceased kings."

A similar find was made as early as 1896 by Edward H. Thompson, the U.S. Consul in Yucatán and one of the early explorers of the great Mayan city of Chichén Itzá. Among the ruins of Chichén Itzá Thompson discovered a small pyramid containing the bones of seven human skeletons, and a cave housing a tomb.

The Egyptian connection does not end there. One of the most brilliant sites of American civilization, built by a people who apparently had close ties with the Mayas, is a city known by its Aztec name of Teotihuacán. It is an extraordinary place near Mexico City, consisting of a vast complex of ruins that were already overgrown when the Spaniards reached America. It is dominated by pyramids, one dedicated to the sun and another to the moon. The base of the sun pyramid measures 740 feet by 725 feet—exactly the same as the base of the Cheops pyramid in Egypt. The height of the Mexican structure is 215 feet, half that of the Egyptian one. Again we have to ask if this is just a strange coincidence or does it have tremendous significance?

Teotihuacán was a city of 100,000 people. Its streets and houses were laid out to a precise grid plan, and the homes of the wealthy were decorated with paintings and frescoes. The city's major buildings were constructed sometime between A.D. 100 and 300, and Teotihuacán was sacked and burned in A.D. 856 by the Toltecs—contemporaries of the Mayas who later overran much of the Mayan empire in Yucatán.

In the Mayan city of Tikal in Guatemala the pyramids are of a height and steepness that astonished the early explorers. One rises to 230 feet, making it the highest known building in the Americas before the construction of New York's first skyscrapers. And in nearby Uaxactún, the oldest Mayan city yet excavated, archaeologists discovered a feature unique in the world: a pyramid within a pyramid.

The Mayas erected *stelae*—carved stone columns—bearing inscriptions that recorded important events. At Tikal a series of stelae was raised to mark the passage of each 20 years between A.D. 629 and 790. On each was the date, the age of the moon, and symbols of the gods ruling at the time. Stelae are not unique to the Mayas. They are an Asian device that the Egyptians, Greeks, and Romans also used.

One of the greatest puzzles about the past is how so many ancient peoples, without our modern technical aids, were able to transport massive building stones over great distances, fashion them precisely, and erect them with such ability that they have stood for thousands of years. The island of Malta in the Mediterranean, for example, is rich in megalithic remains. The primitive men who erected Malta's giant monuments also dug large underground tunnel networks and subterranean chambers. We do not know who these people were or why they carried out this work. Stonehenge is perhaps the most famous example of Stone Age skill that is beyond our comprehension. This ancient circle of stones in Southern England, built about 1800 B.C., attracts a quarter of a million visitors a year. "We today can name no man or tribe who had all these qualifications [to erect the stones] at any time in the period of British prehistory," says the official

Below: this jade mosaic funerary mask covered the face of the man whose skeleton was found in the Funerary Crypt of the Temple of the Inscriptions at Palenque. The eyes were made of shell and obsidian, and the whole fastened to a wooden backing that had rotted away before the tomb was found.

guide to Stonehenge. A recent theory suggests that a party of Egyptians was responsible for its construction because a basic measurement used by its builders was also used by the Egyptians. It is widely believed that the builders of Stonehenge, whoever they were, possessed a considerable knowledge of astronomy. We find a similar knowledge among the peoples of Central America.

In the opinion of French historian Raymond Cartier, "In many fields of knowledge the Mayas outclassed the Greeks and Romans. They were expert astronomers and mathematicians, and thus brought to perfection the science of chronology. They built domed observatories with a more exact orientation than those of 17th-century Paris, e.g. the Caracol erected on three terraces in Chichén Itzá. They had a precise calendar based on a "sacred year" of 260 days, a solar year of 365 days, and a Venusian year of 584 days. The exact length of the solar year has been fixed, after long calculation, at 365·2422 days; the Mayas estimated it at 365·2420 days, i.e. correct to three places of decimals."

The Mayas showed astonishing mathematical skill. While the Romans were still using a cumbersome method of counting, the Mayas invented a system of numbering that has all the features of modern arithmetic. Yet they used only three symbols: a bar for the number five, dots for each unit up to four, and a stylized shell for zero. Above all, the Mayas developed a form of picture-writing, based on a similar system to that used in Egyptian hieroglyphs. Because Diego de Landa, a Spanish monk who became Bishop of Yucatán, burned all the Mayan literature he could lay his hands on, only three Mayan books remain for study, and Mayan writing is still largely undeciphered.

While acknowledging the remarkable achievements of the early American civilizations and their striking similarities to Old World cultures, it is only fair that we also consider the features they did *not* share with Old World civilizations. They had no plow, very few metal tools, no Old World diseases, no Old World domestic animals, and no wheels—except on toys. Indeed it is one of the great mysteries of the American cultures that they never extended the use of wheels from toys to full-size vehicles. Atlantologists and other diffusionists make much of the supposed resemblances between Mayan and ancient Egyptian writing, but although the two scripts are based on similar principles, the signs and language are completely different. Those who argue that the early American civilizations developed under the influence of a greater people, such as the Atlanteans or the Egyptians, must explain all these anomalies.

Probably the most important objection to the theory that Atlantean refugees founded the cultures of the Americas is the enormous time lag between the date given by Plato for the destruction of Atlantis and the emergence of the civilizations of the Olmecs and Mayas, let alone those of the Aztecs and Incas. Either we must believe, like Lewis Spence and others, that the Atlanteans escaped to another continent and only moved on to the Americas at a much later stage, or we must accept that these cultures were the echo of others equally great that date back many thousands of years—as some investigators of Tiahuanaco

Above: the Pyramid of the Sun at Teotihuacán near Mexico City. In the early centuries of the Christian era, Teotihuacán was a magnificent metropolis covering an area of more than eight square miles, and ruling an empire including most of what is now Mexico. When European explorers first investigated the city, they discovered that the base of the pyramid is exactly the same size as that of the Pyramid of Cheops in Egypt— 740 by 725 feet—and that it is exactly half as tall. Could this be simply an amazing coincidence, or is it further proof that there were links between the Old and New Worlds thousands of years ago?

maintain. Atlantologists point out that the peoples of the Americas seem to have been content to reproduce the same patterns of art and architecture over and over again, as if they were copying models provided by others, and that they do not seem to have progressed from an advanced starting point. However, orthodox scholars contest the view that the civilizations of the Americas sprang up suddenly, and are convinced that these cultures evolved, albeit rapidly, from more primitive beginnings. Certainly the claim by some Atlantologists that the Mayas derived their peaceful nature from the Atlanteans does not stand up to close examination. The Mayas may not have been as blood-thirsty as the later Aztecs, but they were undoubtedly warlike and they indulged in human sacrifice.

On the other hand we cannot ignore the persistent legends of the ancient American peoples that tell of visits from fair-skinned "gods" with beards who came from across the sea in the mists of prehistory, bringing the Indians the arts of civilization. This

Below left: a page from the *Dresden Codex*, one of only three Mayan books that have survived to the present day. Although Mayan writing is still largely undeci-phered—principally because so few examples exist—we know that this page contains astronomical calcul-ations on the planet Venus. In the opinion of some experts, Mayan astronomy was far in advance of that of the Greeks and Romans; the accuracy and range of Mayan knowledge astounds scholars still. Below: the "Calendar Stone" from the Aztec capital Tenochtitlán, carved with symbols of the days, months, and suns. The Aztecs based their calendar on that of the Mayas.

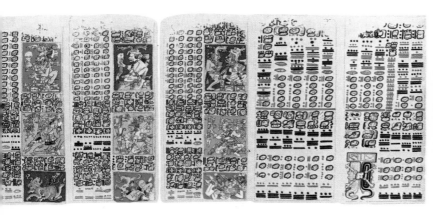

Right: envoys from Aztec emperor Montezuma presenting gifts to the Spanish conquistador Hernando Cortés. Aztec mythology told how the White God Quetzalcoatl had left Mexico, promising one day to return. When the fair-skinned Spaniards reached the Aztec Empire, they were at first mistaken for the returning god, and welcomed by the Aztecs.

Below: Aztec greenstone mask of Quetzalcoatl. Aztec effigies of the White God range from typically Indian ones such as this to representations of men of what appears to be a completely different race. Were they drawn from the artist's imagination or were they based on fact? Were the Americas once visited by travelers from the east?

tradition was common to the Mayas, Aztecs, Incas, and other culturally advanced peoples of pre-Columbian America, though each culture called the White God by a different name. To the Mayas he was Kukulcán; the Toltecs and Aztecs knew him as Quetzalcoatl; and the Incas called him Viracocha.

The discovery of artifacts depicting men with beards and narrow, beaked noses, who look quite un-Indian, appears to some investigators to back up the legends and to provide further evidence that another people influenced American culture. The famous Norwegian anthropologist and diffusionist Thor Heyerdahl is reportedly convinced that "a people, or more exactly a group of men, with fair skin, aquiline noses, and bushy beards exercised a decisive influence on the development of the American civilizations and in particular on those that flourished in the Andes, in ancient Peru."

The legends of the White God were the undoing of these great civilizations, for they welcomed the fair-skinned Spanish conquistadors as gods, and their kingdoms crumbled.

Dr. Michael Coe, a leading expert on Olmec civilization, believes that the earliest site of the Olmecs is in San Lorenzo,

Mexico. Radiocarbon dating of samples from San Lorenzo indicates that the monuments at this site were constructed no later than 900 or 800 B.C., and perhaps considerably earlier. "We have, therefore, found the oldest civilized communities thus far known in Mesoamerica," says Dr. Coe. "Nonetheless, by pushing back the earliest Olmec civilization to such an early date—to a time when there was little else but simple village cultures in the rest of Mexico and Central America—the lack of antecedents is an embarrassing problem. We now have no idea where the Olmec came from or who built the mounds and carved the sculptures of San Lorenzo. Whoever they were, these pioneers must have been unusually gifted in engineering as well as art. . . ."

So, despite attempts to make the civilizations of ancient America appear normal, if remarkable, it seems that there is a mystery that remains unsolved. Perhaps the South American jungles will provide more ruins and more clues. Or perhaps Atlantis will be found, and give us the answers. Unless, of course, the answer lies not in the Atlantic but in the Pacific, in the shape of yet another lost continent.

4

A Lost World in the Pacific

In the evening twilight of Easter Sunday 1722, a Dutch fleet chanced upon a tiny island in the South Pacific—and launched a controversy that has lasted ever since. Admiral Jaakob Roggeveen and his men reached the island too late in the day to explore. They dropped anchor and waited until dawn next day before moving closer to the shore to look for signs of life. At first light they saw a series of small fires on the shore. Then, as the sun climbed slowly above the horizon, an astonishing sight met their eyes. All along the shore, people of different skin colors were apparently worshiping in front of colossal statues.

Right: monumental stone heads brood over the slopes of the extinct volcano Rano Raraku on Easter Island in the Pacific. Similar monoliths line the island's coast and appear to have marked its roads. The men who inhabited Easter Island when European explorers first arrived there could tell their visitors nothing about the construction of the statues. Who sculpted them, and why they were erected, remains one of the greatest mysteries in the world.

65

"The Easter Islanders... seemed to know nothing about their construction"

Roggeveen named the island Paasch Eyland, or Easter Island, because of the day on which his fleet had first sighted it. He and his men spent only a few hours there, but they did take a closer look at the enormous statues. These proved to be huge elongated heads, all very similar and of varying heights. Roggeveen was able to break a piece from one of the statues with his bare fingers and the Dutch explorers concluded it was made from clay and soil mixed with pebbles. In fact, the statues were made from solid rock that had deteriorated with age and erosion. This was discovered by a Spanish expedition under Felipe Gonzalez, which reached the island in 1770. The Spaniards hit the statues with pickaxes, causing sparks to fly.

If the Easter Island statues had been molded, as the Dutch explorers believed, there would have been no mystery. But with the realization that the statues had been hewn from rock a problem arose. How did the inhabitants of this tiny island develop the skill to sculpt the statues and, more important, how did they transport the huge heads and erect them on an island devoid of trees and ropes large enough for the purpose? Later European explorers discovered that, although the Easter Islanders held the statues in awe, they seemed to know nothing about their construction. And as time went by, a new enigma emerged. The Easter Islanders possessed a number of engraved wooden boards, known as *rongorongo* boards or "singing tablets," that appeared to be inscribed with a form of picture-writing. Yet none of the islanders could read the boards with any exactness, and they remain undeciphered. Where did this writing come from? Was it invented by the statue-builders? Is it really writing at all? These and other questions about the perplexing Easter Island civilization have exercised the minds of scholars for 200 years.

Easter Island is dominated by three extinct volcanoes, Rano Raraku, Rano Kao, and Rano Aroi. It is only 13 miles long and 7 miles across at its widest points, and it rises out of the South Pacific in splendid isolation. Its nearest inhabited neighbor is Pitcairn Island—refuge of the *Bounty* mutineers—1200 miles to the west. In the opposite direction, 2300 miles of open ocean lie between Easter Island and the coast of northern Chile.

Yet a people settled on this barren stretch of land, with its boulder-strewn landscape and porous soil. There are no fresh-water rivers or streams and the strong, salt-laden winds prevent the growth of tall plants or trees. There was no animal life to hunt, and life for the early settlers must have been arduous in the extreme. But they multiplied, and apparently developed (or had brought with them) a form of writing. They built roads, temples, and a solar observatory, and carved some 600 massive stone heads with elongated ears. Many of these statues were set up along the coast of the island. Some were erected on the slopes of Rano Raraku, and others appear to have marked the island's roads. The largest of the coastal statues is 33 feet high and weighs 80 tons. It was once surmounted by a 12-ton cylindrical topknot, carved from red stone and measuring six feet high by eight feet wide.

It is hardly surprising, then, that Easter Island has figured prominently in numerous theories about the earth's early civilizations and their origins, particularly as the island's

Above: French explorer Jean de la Pérouse's expedition visits Easter Island in the 1780s. At that time the statues were still surmounted by the red stone topknots that have now fallen off. The statues baffled all the early explorers, who could not understand how a people whose main skill seemed to be as thieves had been able to sculpt and erect these huge heads.

Left: part of a cast of an Easter Island rongorongo board, inscribed with what appears to be picture writing. Early explorers found that the Easter Islanders could not read the boards. Like the stone heads, they seem to be relics of a civilization of the distant past.

MAYAGLYPHS DELANDA'S ALPHABET		CRETAN SCRIPT LINEAR A		

Above: Mayan alphabet, set down by Diego de Landa, 16th-century Spanish Bishop of Yucatán. French cleric Brasseur used de Landa's alphabet to translate the Mayan *Troano Codex*; his translation told of a land called Mu that had sunk beneath the sea. Other theorists compared de Landa's alphabet with Cretan Linear A script to prove a connection between the two lands.

inhabitants at the time of its discovery—who bore no resemblance to the stone colossi—seemed as mystified by the statues as the visitors. Nearly 200 stone heads, including one 66 feet high, are still in the quarry, suddenly abandoned during production, adding one more intriguing element to the enigma.

In the absence of any immediate acceptable solution to the Easter Island problem, scholars and visionaries have been free to give their imagination full rein in an attempt to find the answer. Many have speculated that the island is either part of a sunken Pacific continent, or an outpost of such a lost land. Inevitably, because the Americas sit between the Atlantic and Pacific oceans, much of the "evidence" for a lost Atlantic continent that influenced the cultures of ancient America has been offered in support of a vanished Pacific civilization, also supposed to have carried its arts and skills to the American Indians.

In 1864 a French scholar, the Abbé Charles-Étienne Brasseur de Bourbourg, came across an abridged copy of a treatise on the Mayan civilization in the library of the Historical Academy of Madrid. This treatise, entitled *Account of the Affairs of Yucatán*, had been written by Diego de Landa, the Spanish Bishop of Yucatán, who destroyed all but three books of the Mayans' extensive literature and substituted Christian teachings. After this appalling act of vandalism de Landa became interested in the Mayan culture and tried to learn Mayan writing—a complicated system combining ideographic signs and phonetic elements to produce word-glyphs. As a result he compiled a "Mayan alphabet" and included it in his treatise.

The discovery of this alphabet excited Brasseur. He already had a considerable interest in the civilizations of the New World, and he believed he could use de Landa's alphabet to decipher the three surviving Mayan books. Armed with the alphabet and aided by a lively imagination, he immediately set about translating one of the books, the *Troano Codex*—half of the two-part *Tro-Cortesianus Codex* preserved in Madrid. Soon he revealed that the book told of a volcanic catastrophe and of a land that sank beneath the waves. But there were two symbols in the Mayan manuscript that Brasseur was unable to account for. They bore a very faint resemblance to de Landa's "M" and "U," so he put them together and produced Mu—the name he gave to the submerged land.

Naturally, Brasseur's discovery of the de Landa alphabet caused excitement among historians and scholars, but this quickly turned to disappointment when attempts to translate other Mayan writing with this "key" produced incoherent nonsense. To this day only about one third of the Mayan glyphs are understood, but enough is now known about the language to assert that the *Troano Codex* deals with astrology and not with the destruction of Mu. The other two books—the *Dresden Codex* and the *Codex Perezianus*, preserved in Dresden and Paris respectively—appear to concern astronomy and religious ritual. Although de Landa's alphabet has been shown to be based on erroneous principles, and Brasseur's translation has been discredited, the story of Mu has survived and grown, as others have sought to prove the existence of a lost continent,

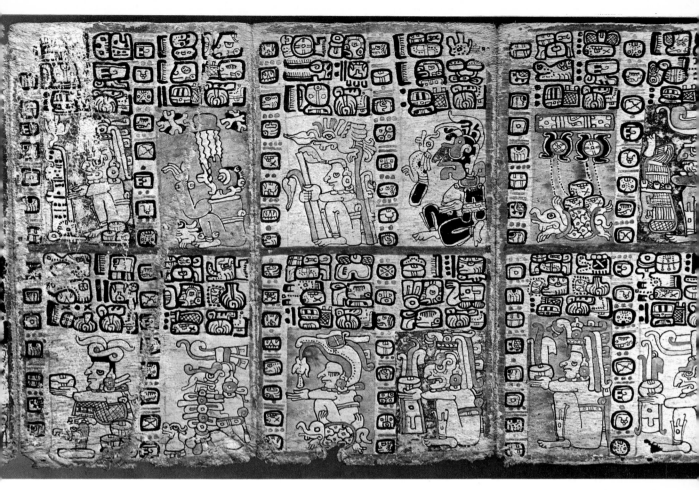

using the same tools. Whereas Brasseur believed Mu to be the name once used for Atlantis, others have adopted it for a South Pacific continent.

Brasseur's contemporary and fellow countryman Augustus Le Plongeon, a physician and archaeologist of some repute, was the first man to excavate Mayan ruins in Yucatán, where he and his American wife Alice lived for many years. Le Plongeon, a resplendent figure with a waist-length beard, attempted his own translation of the *Troano Codex*, drawing a good deal of his inspiration from the work of Brasseur and from a liberal interpretation of pictures found on the walls of ruins in the Mayan city of Chichén-Itzá. Le Plongeon's "translation" retraced the story of the sunken continent of Mu with an extravagance that made Brasseur's account pale in comparison. At the heart of his account is the rivalry of two Muvian princes, Coh and Aac, for the hand of their sister Moo, the Queen of Mu. Prince Coh won, but was killed by his jealous brother who immediately took over the country from Queen Moo.

At the height of this drama, the continent began to sink. Moo fled to Egypt, where she built the Sphinx as a memorial to Prince Coh, and, under the name of Isis, founded the Egyptian civilization. Other Muvians escaped from their sinking homeland to Yucatán, where they recorded their history and erected temples to their leaders. Le Plongeon claimed that Egyptian hieroglyphs

Above: section from the Mayan *Troano Codex,* which is preserved in Madrid. We know today that the *Troano Codex* is concerned with astrology, but in Brasseur's version it appears to suggest the existence of a lost civilization. His translation includes elements of the Atlantis legend—volcanic catastrophe, and the disappearance of the civilization under the sea.

Right: Augustus Le Plongeon, the French archaeologist who was the first to excavate the Mayan ruins in Yucatán. Le Plongeon made his own translation of the *Troano Codex*, based on Brasseur's version and on Mayan pictures he had discovered at Chichén Itzá. His translation is a colorful account of the history of the lost Mu, in which he suggests that Muvians were the ancestors of both the Mayas and the ancient Egyptians. Far right: Le Plongeon's wife Alice.

and Mayan writing were alike—a belief not shared by the specialists in these languages—and even maintained that Jesus spoke Mayan on the Cross.

In the 1880s Augustus and Alice Le Plongeon settled down in Brooklyn to write several books on their experiences and discoveries. The best-known of these was Le Plongeon's *Queen Moo and the Egyptian Sphinx*—published in 1896 and still in print—which included the author's claim to have found the charred entrails of Prince Coh, preserved in a stone urn, during his excavations of Mayan ruins.

Le Plongeon's "translation" of the *Troano Codex* was far more readable—if no more reliable—than Brasseur's. Here is the part of Le Plongeon's version that deals with the destruction of Mu: "In the year 6 Kan, on the 11th Muluc in the month Zac, there occurred terrible earthquakes, which continued without interruption until the 13th Chuen. The country of the hills of mud, the land of Mu was sacrificed; being twice upheaved it suddenly disappeared during the night, the basin being continually shaken by the volcanic forces. Being confined, these caused the land to sink and to rise several times in various places. At last the surface gave way and ten countries were torn asunder and scattered. Unable to stand the force of the convulsion, they sank with their 64,000,000 inhabitants 8060 years before the writing of this book."

According to the Frenchman, he found records in Yucatán stating that "the Hieratic head [high priest] of the land of Mu prophesied its destruction, and that some, heeding the prophecy, left and went to the colonies where they were saved."

Like Brasseur, Le Plongeon believed that Mu and Atlantis were one and the same land. Basing his argument on his interpretations of Mayan wall paintings and inscriptions, he placed the sunken continent in the region of the Gulf of Mexico and the Caribbean Sea, to the East of Central America.

At about the same time, another Frenchman, Louis Jacolliot, was also writing about a lost continent. He had a new name for it, Rutas, and a new source, a collection of Sanskrit myths collected during a stay in India. According to Jacolliot, these myths told of a land named Rutas that sank in the Indian Ocean. But he interpreted them as referring to a Pacific landmass that formerly covered the region now occupied by the Polynesian islands. Plato's Atlantis story, he argued, was merely an echo of this

tremendous event, and the sinking of Rutas caused India and other lands to rise from the sea.

From the 1880s onward, support for the existence of a lost Pacific continent began to appear with surprising frequency, and from sources that were even more surprising. A New York dentist, Dr. John Ballou Newbrough, claimed angelic inspiration for his account of a vanished land called Pan. Newbrough, a spiritualist medium, published the story of Pan in *Oahspe*, a book allegedly produced by automatic writing (hand writing said to occur without the individual's conscious control). The book was subtitled *A Kosmon Bible in the Words of Jehovah and his Angel Ambassadors*. It was first published in 1882, and has since been largely ridiculed for its misinformation and unfulfilled prophecies.

According to *Oahspe*, man appeared on earth 72,000 years ago as a result of the union between the angels and a species of seal-like animals. Newbrough's book contains a map of the earth in antediluvian times showing the triangular continent of Pan in the north Pacific. Pan sank beneath the waves 24,000 years ago. However, it is scheduled to rise again in the very near future. *Oahspe* tells us that Pan will begin to resurface in 1980, and when its cities and the records of its civilization are finally exposed we will have no difficulty in deciphering its books or learning about its culture, because *Oahspe* very thoughtfully supplies us with a Panic dictionary and a Panic alphabet.

Not all proponents of a lost Pacific continent needed the help of angels to formulate their ideas. A New Zealander, Professor

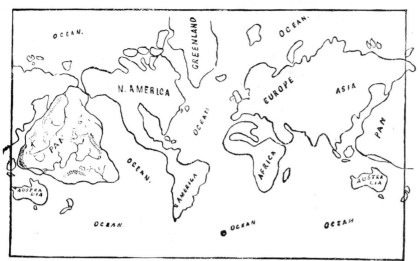

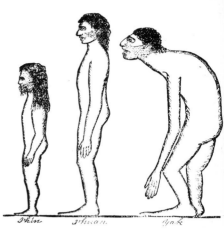

J. MacMillan Brown, drew upon his knowledge of geology, archaeology, and anthropology to explain the mystery of Easter Island. He argued that there had once been either a continent or a densely populated archipelago in the South Pacific, inhabited by white men, and that Easter Island had served as a collective burial ground for the people of neighboring islands. The professor pointed to similarities between the monuments and customs of the Polynesian people and those of the Peruvian civilizations, believing that South American culture had reached that continent from the west. Although Professor Brown has been described as "a man with a mind both simple and excessively imaginative," parts of his theory find support today in a new interpretation of Polynesian culture by modern experts.

The professor published his theory in the form of a book, *Riddle of the Pacific*, which appeared in 1906. Shortly afterward, between 1908 and 1926, the German explorer Leo Frobenius made discoveries in Yorubaland—part of Nigeria—that led him to believe he had discovered Atlantis. He identified the Nigerian god Olokon with Poseidon, and argued that the Yoruba culture contained many elements, such as the short bow and tattooing, that he said were non-African. He went on to state his belief that civilization had begun on a lost Pacific continent. It had spread from there to Asia, then to the west, giving rise to the Egyptian and Atlanto-Nigerian civilizations.

All these protagonists had merely set the stage for the appearance of the most outrageous supporter of a vanished Pacific continent. James Churchward, a small, thin Anglo-American, was in his seventies when he first revealed the results of a lifetime's research on the subject. His first book, *The Lost Continent of Mu*, published in 1926, made fascinating reading, though acceptance of its contents demands a high degree of gullibility on the part of the reader. Nevertheless, Churchward's name is now almost synonymous with Mu's, and his book is still in print.

Churchward based his theory on two sets of tablets, one of which no one has had the privilege of studying except a priest in whose temple the tablets were allegedly preserved. In his first book Churchward claims to have seen these "Naacal tablets" in an Indian temple; elsewhere he says he studied them in Tibet.

The other set of tablets is a collection of some 2500 stone objects found in Mexico by an American engineer named William Niven. These objects, which look like flattened figurines, were made in great numbers by the Aztecs and other Mexican peoples. No one else seemed to think there was anything on them worth deciphering, but Churchward claimed to be able to "read" their bumps and curlicues. They are symbols that originated in Mu, he said, and they convey deep and mysterious meanings. He dated the Niven tablets as at least 12,000 years old, and claimed that they and the Naacal tablets contain extracts from the Sacred Inspired Writings of Mu.

Churchward's first book begins with these compelling words: "The Garden of Eden was not in Asia but on a now sunken continent in the Pacific Ocean. The Biblical story of creation—the epic of the seven days and the seven nights—came first not from the peoples of the Nile or of the Euphrates Valley but from this now submerged continent, Mu—the Motherland of Man.

"These assertions can be proved by the complex records I discovered upon long-forgotten sacred tablets in India, together with records from other countries. They tell of this strange country of 64,000,000 inhabitants, who, 50,000 years ago, had developed a civilization superior in many respects to our own. They described, among other things, the creation of man in the mysterious land of Mu."

Below: painting by James Churchward from his book on Mu, which he described as a continent in the central Pacific Ocean. He captioned this illustration as "A Volcanic Cataclysm such as completed the destruction of the Maya edifices in Yucatán after the earthquakes had shaken them to their foundations. The Yucatán Maya, the builders, were virtually wiped out. 9500 B.C." As we now know, the Mayas established themselves in Yucatán only after A.D. 700, more than 1600 years after Churchward's date for their fall.

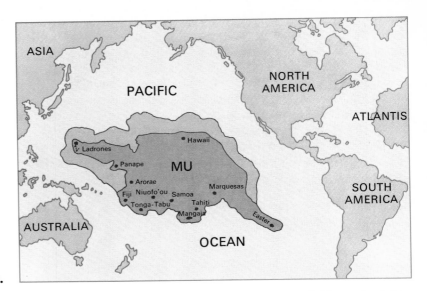

Right: Churchward's map of Mu, covering most of Polynesia in the Pacific Ocean. According to his theory, Mu sank beneath the sea some 13,000 years ago, leaving only the Polynesian islands visible above the waves. The survivors of the cataclysm, crowded onto these small islands, reverted to savagery and became cannibals.

Above: one of the Naacal tablets that Churchward claimed to have discovered in an Indian temple, and from which he learned the history of Mu. This tablet, Churchward explains, tells of the creation of the first man, of his division into man and woman, and of how their progeny peopled the world.

Churchward explains that he saw the sacred Naacal tablets during a stay in India (or Tibet, depending on which of his books we are reading). While he was studying the bas-reliefs in a certain temple, he became friendly with the temple's high priest. He discovered that the man was interested in archaeology and ancient records, "and had a greater knowledge of those subjects than any other living man." The high priest began teaching Churchward how to read the peculiar inscriptions on the temple walls, and Churchward spent the next two years studying this strange language, which "my priestly friend believed to be the original tongue of mankind." Churchward learned that only two other priests in India knew this language.

Interpreting the temple writings proved difficult, because many apparently simple inscriptions had hidden meaning, "which had been designed especially for the Holy Brothers— the Naacals—a priestly brotherhood sent from the motherland [Mu] to the colonies to teach the sacred writings, religion, and the sciences." One day, in the course of a conversation with Churchward, the priest revealed that there were a number of ancient tablets in the temple's secret archives, which were believed to have originated either in Burma or in the vanished land of Mu itself. He had never seen the tablets, only the containers in which they were kept. Although he was in a position to examine the tablets, the high priest had not done so because they were sacred records not to be touched.

Churchward argued that the tablets might not be packed away properly and could be deteriorating, a view that the priest eventually shared, and so the containers were opened. According to Churchward the tablets, written in the same dead language that he had been studying, described in detail the earth's creation, the appearance of man, and the land on which he evolved—Mu.

Having learned that more tablets were preserved in other Indian temples, Churchward set off on an unsuccessful quest for them. He then turned to a study of the writings of old civilizations, which confirmed his belief that the Chaldeans, Babylonians, Persians, Egyptians, Greeks, and Hindus had been preceded by the civilization of Mu.

"Continuing my researches, I discovered that this lost continent had extended from somewhere north of Hawaii to the south as far as the Fijis and Easter Island, and was undoubtedly the original habitat of man. I learned that in this beautiful country there had lived a people that colonized the earth, and that the land had been obliterated by terrific earthquakes and submersion 12,000 years ago, and had vanished in a vortex of fire and water."

According to Churchward, Mu was a beautiful, tropical country with vast plains covered with rich grazing grasses and tilled fields. There were no mountains, "for mountains had not yet been forced up from the bowels of the earth," but there were low, rolling hills, shaded by tropical vegetation. Many "broad, slow-running streams and rivers, which wound their sinuous ways in fantastic curves and bends around the wooded hills and through the fertile plains," watered the land and produced luxuriant flowers and shrubs.

Churchward peoples his graphic picture of the vanished continent with gaudy-winged butterflies, humming birds, lively crickets, mighty mastodons and elephants, and a population of 64,000,000 noble human beings enjoying "a gay and happy life."

The inhabitants of Mu consisted of ten tribes all under one government, ruled by an emperor, the Ra Mu. "The dominant race in the land of Mu was a white race, exceedingly handsome people, with clear white or olive skins, large, soft, dark eyes, and straight black hair. Besides this white race, there were other races, people with yellow, brown, or black skins. They, however, did not dominate."

The Muvians built broad, smooth roads running in all directions like a spider's web, and the stones from which the roads were constructed were matched so perfectly that not a blade of grass could grow between them. They were great navigators, and they made all the other countries on the planet their colonies. It was an idyllic life, and on cool evenings pleasure ships, filled with gorgeously dressed, jewel-bedecked men and women, rejoiced at their good fortune. "While this great land was thus at its zenith," Churchward's account continues, "center of the earth's civilization, learning, trade and commerce, with great stone temples being erected, and huge statues and monoliths set up, she received a rude shock; a fearful visitation overtook her."

Earthquakes and volcanic eruptions shook the southern parts of the continent, destroying many cities. Tidal waves flooded the land, and the lava piled up into high cones that are still to be seen today in the form of the Pacific Islands. Eventually the Muvians were able to rebuild these cities, and life returned to normal. Then, many generations later, a similar but far greater catastrophe struck Mu, and "the whole continent heaved and rolled like the ocean's waves." Churchward is not one to miss the drama of such an event. "With thunderous roarings the doomed land sank," he writes. "Down, down, down she went, into the mouth of hell—'a tank of fire'." Then 50 million square miles of water poured over the continent, drowning the vast majority of its noble inhabitants.

The only visible remains of the great continent were its lava

Above: Princess Arawali of Arorai Island in the Gilbert group. This photograph was reproduced in Churchward's book to prove the descent of the Pacific islanders from the inhabitants of Mu. The fan Arawali carries, Churchward asserts, is ornamented with the royal escutcheon of Mu.

cones, which formed chains of small islands, covered to capacity with the survivors of the cataclysm. With no clothing, no tools, no shelter, and no food, these formerly peace-loving people had to become cannibals in order to survive. The colonies that Mu had founded continued for a while, but without the help of the motherland they eventually flickered out. Churchward asserts that Atlantis was one of these colonies, and suffered a similar fate to Mu 1000 years later.

Churchward claimed that his findings solved the mysteries surrounding the first inhabitants of the South Sea Islands and the origins of the ancient American civilizations. "On some of the South Sea Islands, notably Easter, Mangaia, Tongatabu, Panape, and the Ladrone or Marianas Islands," he writes, "there stand today vestiges of old stone temples and other lithic [stone] remains that take us back to the time of Mu. At Uxmal, in Yucatán, a ruined temple bears inscriptions commemorative of the 'Lands of the West, whence we came'; and the striking Mexican pyramid southwest of Mexico City, according to its inscriptions, was raised as a monument to the destruction of these same 'Lands of the West'."

Even those readers prepared to believe that Churchward was privileged to see the ancient Naacal tablets may wonder how he was able to decipher them—and the Niven tablets that also supplied part of his story—so quickly. However, Churchward has an explanation for this. Like many occultists, he believed that it is possible for a suitably gifted person to decipher the secret language of symbols (said to have been used by all the ancients to record their wisdom) simply by staring at the symbols until their meaning emerges from the student's inner consciousness. It was this technique, in which he was aided by the teachings of the Indian (or Tibetan) high priest, that enabled Churchward to recover the forgotten history of Mu.

In considering the possibility that there was once a huge continent in the Pacific, we need to take a fresh look at the islands now occupying that area. The place deserving the closest scrutiny is undoubtedly Easter Island with its huge sculptures and associated mysteries. Why did the people of such a tiny island build so many very similar stone heads? Why, instead of carving them one at a time, were they producing as many as 200 simultaneously in their quarry when they suddenly abandoned their work?

Some have suggested that the island was part of Mu, and the place at which the stone monuments were carved before being transported to other parts of the continent. Others believe Easter Island to have been a burial ground, a sacred area of Mu that became an island when the rest of the continent sank.

The man who has done most in our time to popularize Easter Island and to solve its riddles is Thor Heyerdahl, the Norwegian anthropologist who, in 1947, led the famous Scandinavian *Kon-Tiki* expedition from South America to Polynesia. He subsequently organized expeditions to the Galápagos Islands in 1952 and to Easter Island in 1955. Heyerdahl is convinced that all the Polynesian islands were originally settled by people from South America. When he first published his theory, in 1941, most scientists disregarded the possibility of South American in-

Right: Churchward's painting of the submersion of Mu. He wrote that *"the whole continent* heaved and rolled like the ocean's waves. The land trembled and shook like the leaves of a tree in a storm. Temples and palaces came crashing to the ground. . . ."* That night, the continent broke up and was engulfed first by fire, then by the waves.

Below: drawing by Churchward of "the probable condition underlying Mu before her submersion." The earth beneath the continent, Churchward stated, was honeycombed with chambers filled with explosive volcanic gases. Pressure caused cracks and fissures in the rocks, and the gases escaped upward, leaving the chambers empty behind them. With no "bolstering gases" to support their roofs, they collapsed and Mu sank beneath the sea.

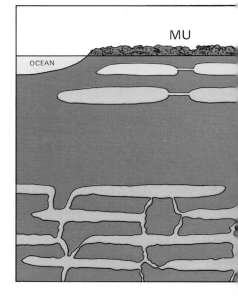

Right: North American Indian picture, interpreted by Churchward as an illustration of the destruction of the continent of Mu. The picture is surmounted by the plumed serpent, which—according to Churchward—is God of Creation. Beneath the serpent, the Thunder Bird, symbolizing the creative forces, holds in its talons the Killer Whale, the ocean waters. But the whale is dead, indicating that the waters have completed the catastrophic destruction of Mu.

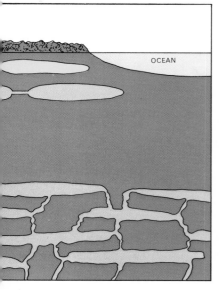

fluence on Polynesia because of the vast expanse of ocean that lies between South America and the nearest South Pacific islands. It seemed unlikely, to say the least, that the South American Indians with their frail reed and balsa wood craft could have crossed thousands of miles of ocean to carry their culture to Polynesia. Most authorities believed that the Polynesians had come from the other direction, from Asia. Heyerdahl agreed that Asian immigrants *had* reached the Polynesian islands, but he was convinced that they were preceded by colonizers from South America.

To help prove his case, Heyerdahl and his team built the balsa wood raft *Kon-Tiki* based on the traditional materials and techniques used in the construction of South American boats. In 1947, he and five companions set out aboard the raft from Callao, Peru. They spent 101 days at sea, allowing the South Equatorial Current and the prevailing trade winds to carry them 4300 nautical miles to the little Polynesian atoll of Raroia in the Tuamotu Archipelago.

The voyage made Heyerdahl famous, but many scientists remained skeptical. To show a thing can be done is not the same as proving it was done, said the critics. And even if people from South America had reached Polynesia, this did not prove that there was regular contact across the ocean or that the sailors from Peru founded the culture of the Polynesian islands, as Heyerdahl suggested. Orthodox scientists were even more outraged when Heyerdahl suggested that the civilizers from Peru might have been the fair-skinned, bearded men enshrined in Indian legend, who had previously influenced the development of the American civilizations.

However, Heyerdahl is a careful scientist, and he has carried out a great deal of research among the American Indians and the Polynesians in order to provide evidence for his theories. His

Left: one of the giant Easter Island statues, its red topknot restored by archaeologists, gazes over the Pacific landscape as it first did hundreds of years ago. Some believe that these statues are all that remains of an ancient Pacific civilization and that Easter Island was part of a landmass that has sunk beneath the waves. Right: Thor Heyerdahl (left) with historian Bjørn Landström. Heyerdahl has done more than anyone to solve the mystery of Easter Island.

expedition to Easter Island in 1955 was the first to undertake a thorough archaeological study, including modern techniques such as radiocarbon dating, and he combined his examination of the island's past with a practical approach to such problems as how the Easter Island statues were transported.

Why is it that Easter Island, the most remote and inaccessible of all the countless Polynesian islands, should be the very one among them to possess the most abundant and spectacular archaeological remains? And why, alone in Polynesia, should it have a system of writing? asked Heyerdahl. He believed that the key to these questions lay in the island's situation. Of all the inhabited Polynesian islands, Easter Island is the nearest to South America—and the farthest from Asia. It is likely to have been

Above: the balsa-wood raft *Kon-Tiki* nears the end of its 4300-mile drift across the Pacific from Peru to the Tuamotu Islands. The voyage was undertaken by Heyerdahl and five companions to try to prove Heyerdahl's theory that Polynesia was first colonized from the Americas, not from Asia. He believes that civilization reached Easter Island from the same source. Right: long-eared Easter Islander in the 1770s. The Peruvian Indians also elongated their ears like this.

the first island colonized by settlers from South America, whereas migrants from Asia would have reached it last.

Heyerdahl's excavations, backed up by radiocarbon dating tests, showed that a considerable population lived on Easter Island around A.D. 380—about 1000 years earlier than anyone had hitherto suspected. Heyerdahl believes that these people came from Peru, bringing with them their stoneworking techniques. They built temples, roads, and a solar observatory that resemble the magnificent constructions found in ancient Peru. Their temples were astronomically oriented, altarlike elevations, evidently built by specialized stonemasons.

This cultural period was succeeded by another around A.D. 1100, when a new wave of immigrants overran the island. These people showed similar—but not identical—stone-carving skills to their predecessors, and Heyerdahl believes that they too came from Peru. It was during this period that the giant statues were carved and placed on terraced stone platforms that contained burial vaults. The huge heads, depicting long-eared men, recall the practice among the Inca and other Peruvian Indians of elongating the ears by inserting ornamental plugs into the lobes.

According to Heyerdahl, the statue-builders controlled the island for nearly 600 years, but around 1680 the production of statues stopped abruptly, and from then on the giant heads were gradually toppled or destroyed. In Heyerdahl's view, this occurred as the result of another invasion of the island, this time by Polynesians arriving from the direction of Asia. Archaeological evidence suggests that from about 1680 onward the island underwent a period of decadence and warfare, and Easter Island legends tell of a lengthy conflict between "the short ears" (whom Heyerdahl identifies with the Polynesian invaders) and "the long ears" (the statue-builders). The "short ears" eventually won, wiping out the "long ears" and destroying their civilization. The Polynesians were left in control of the island, unable to carve the statues or read the rongorongo boards left by their predecessors. Apart from the remaining statues, the only picture we now have of the earlier settlers is the wood carving, produced by the hundred for commercial purposes by today's Easter Islanders. It shows an emaciated person with goatee beard, aquiline nose, and long ear-lobes. The islanders claim that these were the people their ancestors found and exterminated.

Apart from the early date ascribed to Easter Island civilization, one of the most remarkable discoveries made by Heyerdahl was that when the first settlers arrived on Easter Island there were trees in abundance. The settlers had to cut them down in order to clear the way for the transportation of stones from the quarry. The trees were still there when the statue-builders arrived. Thus the means of moving and erecting the giant statues is no longer a mystery. Indeed Heyerdahl arranged for some of the present-day inhabitants to erect a fallen statue by levering it up with long poles and ropes and gradually blocking piles of small rocks underneath it. It took 12 men 18 days to raise the 25-ton statue—but they did it.

Heyerdahl still has his detractors. Critics point out that, despite the apparent similarities between the stoneworking techniques of Easter Island and Peru, there are fundamental differences between the two. The Easter Islanders built rubble walls that they faced with thin slabs of stone, whereas the Peruvians built with solid blocks of stone. What is more, the Peruvians could not have brought writing to Easter Island, because they themselves had no written language. Indeed, many scholars believe that the inscriptions on the rongorongo boards are not, strictly speaking, a system of writing at all, but rather a device to jog the memory of the storytellers or hymn-singers who used the symbols as reminders of the key elements of their story when reciting lengthy ritual chants. Above all, the critics attack Heyerdahl's use of legend to support his theories, because the legends themselves are often contradictory. They also point out that the Easter Islanders and the Peruvian Indians were not alone in elongating their ear-lobes. This practice is also found in Polynesian islands much closer to Asia.

Nevertheless, Heyerdahl's tireless endeavors in support of his claims and his undoubted contribution to our knowledge of Easter Island have led to a reevaluation of the idea of cultural contact between South America and Polynesia, and a number of scientists now accept at least part of his theory concerning the history of Easter Island.

Heyerdahl has shown that it is possible to explain the mysteries of Easter Island without recourse to a lost continent. But

Top: inserting long poles under a fallen statue prior to raising it. One of the greatest mysteries of the Easter Island statues was how the men who made them moved and raised them on an island without trees. During his 1955 expedition to the island, Heyerdahl discovered that it had once been thickly wooded. The first problem was solved. Above: poles act as levers, while stones are piled under the statue.

Above: the heap of stones under the statue gradually grows until the great head is almost vertical. At this stage, ropes are used to prevent it toppling over. It took 12 men 18 days to raise the statue using only these primitive tools.
Left: Heyerdahl and an islander in front of the newly raised head. Heyerdahl's work showed how the sculptures could have been erected, and his theories might explain their existence without the need for a "lost continent". If Polynesia was settled from the Americas, Easter Island is the first land travelers would have reached.

even if his claims are correct, they need not mean that such a continent never existed in the Pacific. If the continent sank 12,000 years ago, as Churchward maintained, it could well have taken all evidence of its existence with it. Easter Island may be one of its peaks, even if the cultures whose remains now litter its surface appear to have no connection with Mu.

The Pacific region seems so rich in unsolved mysteries and enigmatic finds that almost any theorist, however outlandish, will probably find some "evidence" for his ideas in this part of the globe. Until a more thorough archaeological examination of the area has been carried out, it would be unwise to jump to any firm conclusions. After all, in many ways the huge Pacific Ocean—the world's largest at 68,000,000 square miles—with its volcanic history and strings of islands, might seem to be a more promising site for a vanished continent than the much smaller Atlantic (31,830,000 square miles).

Lemuria
–the Missing
Link?

The descendants of a long-lost race from a vanished continent are alive and well and living on the slopes of Mount Shasta in northern California. So claimed an article in the *Los Angeles Times Star* of May 22, 1932. The writer of the article, reporter Edward Lanser, said he had first learned about these people while traveling at night on the *Shasta Limited*, the train taking him to Portland, Oregon. From the train's observation car Lanser had seen strange red and green lights illuminating Mount Shasta. The conductor of the train told him that these were the work of "Lemurians holding ceremonials." Understandably intrigued, and sensing a scoop

Right: the ring-tailed lemur, from a German work on natural history published in 1775. The lemur, a small mammal related to man, is found principally in Madagascar, but lives too in other countries bordering the Indian Ocean. In the 19th century, those who accepted Charles Darwin's theory of the evolution of species found it difficult to explain how the lemur had reached these countries, separated as they are by wide expanses of sea. It was suggested that the lemur's homelands might once have been connected by a continent that has now vanished. The continent was named Lemuria, for the animal whose existence made it necessary.

Lemur Catta Linn.

"One man had become an expert on this strange Lemurian settlement"

for his newspaper, Lanser made an expedition into the Mount Shasta wilderness in search of these mysterious beings, said to be the last descendants of the earth's first inhabitants.

Lanser drove to the town of Weed where he heard tell of a "mystic village" on Mount Shasta and talked to other investigators who had seen the Lemurians' ceremonial lights, during the daytime as well as at night. But no one had ever been able to enter the "sacred precincts" of the Mount Shasta colony—or if they had, they had not returned to tell the tale. One man, however, had managed to become an expert on this strange Lemurian settlement: "the eminent scientist Professor Edgar Lucin Larkin." According to Lanser, Professor Larkin, "with determined sagacity, penetrated the Shasta wilderness as far as he could—or dared—and then, cleverly, continued his investigations from a promontory with a powerful long-distance telescope."

Peering through his telescope the professor had seen a great temple in the midst of the Lemurian village. It was a splendid piece of architecture, carved from marble and onyx, which rivaled the beauty of the magnificent Mayan temples in Yucatán. Although the investigators seemed frightened to trespass on the Lemurians' sacred terrain, the evidence was that they were a peace-loving, friendly community, apparently leading the same kind of life as their ancestors had done before their homeland sank beneath the sea.

Lanser reported that the people of Weed had occasionally met Lemurians and were able to give a good description of them.

They were "tall, barefoot, noble-looking men, with close-cropped hair, dressed in spotless white robes." The town's storekeepers had good reason to like them. The Lemurians purchased huge quantities of sulfur, salt, and lard, paying with large gold nuggets—worth far more than the merchandise—that they apparently mined from Mount Shasta.

How had this ancient people been able to remain undetected for so long? Lanser provided the answer in his remarkable account. The Lemurians, he said, possessed "the secret power of the Tibetan masters," which enabled them to blend with their surroundings and vanish at will, and they encircled their village with an "invisible protective boundary" to keep intruders out. According to Lanser, the Lemurians' scientific knowledge was far greater than ours. And although they had lived in America—which they called Gustama—for several hundred thousand years, they had not forgotten their homeland. Their strangely lit ceremonials on the slopes of Mount Shasta were held in honor of the long-lost Lemuria.

Those readers of the *Los Angeles Times Star* who took Lanser's story without a pinch of salt were to be disappointed. Lanser's report contains the only allegedly eye-witness account of the Mount Shasta Lemurians ever published, and no subsequent investigators have found the mystic village or its strange inhabitants. Either these mysterious people never existed or they have since blended irretrievably into their surroundings. Professor Larkin, who studied the Lemurians through his telescope, turns out to be no "eminent scientist," as Lanser

Below: Mount Shasta in California. In 1932, Mount Shasta was named as the home of a colony of Lemurians in a feature article in the *Los Angeles Star*. According to the writer of the article, the Mount Shasta Lemurians had emigrated to the United States from their homeland in the Indian Ocean. They lived a secluded life on the mountain, but did venture into a local town to buy supplies—although, strangely enough, no one walking on the mountain had ever seen the colony. Not surprisingly, the article was soon proved to be a fraud.

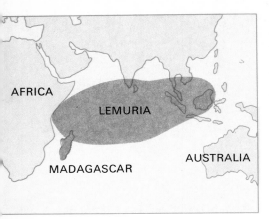

Above: Ernst Haeckel's map of the probable site of Lemuria in the Indian Ocean, joining Madagascar, Africa, India, and the Malay Peninsula—the homelands of the lemur. Naturalist Haeckel, a keen advocate of Darwin's theories, believed an Indian Ocean continent was necessary to explain how the lemur had arrived in its present homes.

claimed, but an elderly occultist who ran the Mount Lowe Observatory in California. Unlike its neighbor, the Mount Wilson Observatory, which is a great scientific institution, the Mount Lowe Observatory was a tourist attraction operated by the Pacific Electric Railway, and Larkin's job was to show visitors the stars through a small telescope. Larkin died in 1924—eight years before the publication of Lanser's article.

Mount Shasta had already been a subject of mystical speculation long before Lanser wrote his Lemurian story. In 1894 a writer named Frederick Spencer Oliver published an occult novel entitled *A Dweller on Two Planets*, under the name "Phylos the Tibetan." In this book the narrator meets his Master, a Chinese named Quong, on Mount Shasta, where sages have established a community to preserve the wisdom of the ancients. Having inducted him into their order, the sages take the narrator to visit Venus in his spiritual body and also teach him to remember his previous incarnations. These include a life on Atlantis, where he rose from miner's son to prince of the realm. He then got involved with two women at once, which proved to be his undoing.

Although we can dismiss the Lanser story as a fascinating piece of fiction based on another piece of fiction, we cannot discard the Lemurians in the same way. Their country of origin, Lemuria, was first suggested in the mid-1800s by scientists trying to account for striking resemblances between the rocks and fossils of Central India and South Africa and for the spread of certain fauna and flora between these continents. One animal that puzzled them particularly was the lemur, a small mammal related to both men and monkeys. The lemur, which looks like a cross between a monkey and a squirrel, lives mainly on the island of Madagascar, but is also found in Africa, India, and the Malay Archipelago.

The debate over the lemur emerged in the wake of Charles Darwin's great thesis on evolution, *On The Origin of Species*, published in 1859. At this time there were two schools of thought: either God had created the various species and put them on earth in the form that we know them, or they had evolved over millions of years. If the former were the case, then God could put His creations wherever He liked—limiting similar species to a particular area of the globe, or placing them on continents thousands of miles apart. But if similar species had evolved in one place from a common ancestor, as Darwin and his supporters thought, the geographical spread of those species had to be in accordance with the limitations of the global picture. In the evolutionists' scheme of things, the lowly lemur presented a problem, because some means had to be found by which it could have crossed the ocean to its present areas of distribution.

Biologists were quick to come up with the obvious solution to the dilemma. The areas now inhabited by the lemur must once have been connected in one vast continent, which still existed at the time when mammals were evolving. The English zoologist Philip L. Sclater suggested that the continent be called "Lemuria" in honor of the lemur.

Many eminent people were ready to accept the possibility of such a continent. Alfred Russel Wallace, who independently

developed the theory of evolution simultaneously with Darwin, wrote: "This is undoubtedly a legitimate and highly probable supposition, and it is an example of the way in which a study of the geographical distribution of animals may enable us to reconstruct the geography of a bygone age. . . . It [Lemuria] represents what was probably a primary zoological region in some past geological epoch; but what that epoch was and what were the limits of the region in question, we are quite unable to say. If we are to suppose that it comprised the whole area now inhabited by Lemuroid animals, we must make it extend from West Africa to Burmah, South China and Celebes, an area which it possibly did once occupy."

Among the most ardent supporters of Lemuria was the German naturalist Ernst Heinrich Haeckel. In a burst of enthusiasm he suggested that if Lemuria had existed it could solve a hotly disputed matter of far greater significance than the spread of the lemurs—namely, the origin of man.

"Of the five now existing continents," Haeckel wrote in the 1870s, "neither Australia nor America nor Europe can have been this primeval home (of man), or the so-called 'Paradise' the 'cradle of the human race.' Besides Southern Asia, the only other of the now existing continents which might be viewed in this light is Africa. But there are a number of circumstances (especially chronological facts), which suggest that the primeval home of man was a continent now sunk below the surface of the Indian Ocean, which extended along the South of Asia, as it is at present (and probably in direct connection with it), towards the east, as far as Further India and the Sunda Islands; towards the west as far as Madagascar and the southeastern shores of Africa. We have already mentioned that many facts in animal and vegetable geography render the former existence of such a South Indian continent very probable. . . . By assuming this Lemuria to have been man's primeval home, we greatly facilitate the explanation of the geographical distribution of the human species by migration."

At the height of the great debate on evolution no fossil remains of man, or of forms intermediate between apes and man, had been identified. (Although fragments of Neanderthal man had already been found, they were only later identified.) Some scientists therefore concluded that the land on which man evolved had disappeared, taking the evidence with it, and Lemuria seemed a good candidate for the site of man's emergence. Our subsequent knowledge of man's family tree and his gradual evolution has done away with the need for a Lemuria-type place of origin, just as other theories have been found to account for the distribution of the lemur, but this information came too late to stop Lemuria taking its place alongside Atlantis and Mu as a great lost continent. No sooner had scientists made the cautious suggestion that Lemuria might have existed than the occultists brought it to life with vivid accounts, derived from supernormal sources, of its inhabitants and their civilization. As a result, Lemuria is now an apparently imperishable feature of the thinking of most leading occult groups.

Madame Helena Petrovna Blavatsky, the greatest of modern occultists and founder of the occult group known as the Theosophical Society, started the ball rolling. In 1888 she published a vast work, *The Secret Doctrine*, which set out her philosophy and gave its readers an insight into the ancient wisdom imparted to her by the Brotherhood of Mahatmas, ethereal beings who were said to run the world from their Tibetan headquarters. Madame Blavatsky maintained that her book was based on an ancient work called the *Book of Dzyan*, which the Mahatmas had shown her during the astral visits they paid her. The *Book of Dzyan*, she says, was written on palm-leaf pages, and had been composed in Atlantis in the now forgotten Senzar language. Besides describing Atlantis it dealt with the lost continent of Lemuria.

It is not easy for the reader to understand the full meaning of Madame Blavatsky's writings, or those of the mysterious *Book of Dzyan* from which she quotes at length. She writes: "After great throes she cast off her old Three and put on her new Seven Skins, and stood in her first one. . . . The Wheel whirled for thirty crores more. It constructed Rûpas; soft Stones that hardened, hard Plants that softened. Visible from invisible, Insects and small Lives. . . ."

Describing the emergence of life on earth, Madame Blavatsky declares that we are the "Fifth Root Race" to inhabit the earth, and that our planet is destined to have seven such races, each composed of seven subraces. The First Root Race, invisible beings made of fire-mist, lived on an Imperishable Sacred Land. The Second, who were just visible, inhabited the former Arctic continent of Hyperborea. The Third Root Race was the Lemurians, gigantic, brainless, apelike creatures. The Fourth Root Race was the fully human Atlanteans, who were destroyed through black magic. We are the Fifth, and the Sixth will evolve from us and return to live on Lemuria. After the Seventh Root Race, life will leave our planet and start afresh on Mercury.

According to Madame Blavatsky, some of the Lemurians had four arms, and some had an eye in the back of their heads, which gave them "psychic vision." They had no spoken language, using telepathy instead as their method of communication. They lived in caves and holes in the ground, and although they had no proper brain they could use their willpower literally to move mountains. Their homeland, Lemuria, occupied practically the whole of the Southern Hemisphere, "from the foot of the Himalayas to within a few degrees of the Antarctic Circle." Although their continent was swept away before the Eocene epoch—which occurred from 60 million to 40 million years ago—their descendants survived to become the Australian Aborigines, Papuans, and Hottentots.

After Madame Blavatsky's death in 1891 her successor, Annie Besant, wrote at length on the subject of Lemuria and its people, as did another leading British Theosophist, W. Scott-Elliot. He put the flesh on the bones of Madame Blavatsky's Lemuria with an astonishing account based on occult revelations he had received from the "Theosophical Masters." He was helped further by having had "the privilege . . . to be allowed to obtain copies—more or less complete" of a set of maps showing the world at critical stages of its history. They form the basis of six world maps reproduced in Scott-Elliot's book *The Story of Atlantis and The Lost Lemuria*, published in 1896 and still kept in print by the Theosophical Society.

Scott-Elliot enlarged on Madame Blavatsky's description of Lemuria. He said that this huge continent took shape when the great northern continent of Hyperborea—his and Madame Blavatsky's designated home of the Second Root Race—broke up. The Manus, the unseen supervisors of the universe, then chose Lemuria for the evolution of the Third Root Race. Their first attempt at producing human life resulted in jellylike creatures, but in time the Lemurians' bodies hardened and they were able to stand up.

From Scott-Elliot's description, the Lemurians were far from beautiful. They were between 12 and 15 feet tall. Their faces were flat, apart from a protruding muzzle, and they had no foreheads. Their skin was brown, and their eyes were set so wide apart that they could see sideways as well as forward. As for the Lemurians' third eye in the back of the head, that now forms the pineal gland in our brains. The capacity to see out of the backs of their heads was particularly useful to the Lemurians, because their heels stuck out so far at the back that they could walk backward as well as forward.

The Lemurians started out as egg-laying hermaphrodites, but

Below: H. P. Blavatsky, founder of the Theosophical Society and an ardent supporter of the Lemuria theory. The existence of Lemuria was first suggested by scientists to explain facts for which no explanation then existed, but it was soon seized on by occultists as a medium for their own mystical ideas. Madame Blavatsky believed that the inhabitants of Lemuria were the third of the seven "root races" into which she divided man.

by the time their fifth subrace evolved they were reproducing as we do. However, during their sexual progress they foolishly interbred with beasts, producing the apes that still populate our planet. This upset the Lhas, supernatural beings whose duty it was, at this stage of the cosmic plan, to incarnate on earth in human bodies to help the evolving Lemurians. So the Lhas refused to carry out their appointed task. Beings from Venus saved the day by offering to take the place of the Lhas. The Venusians—called "Lords of the Flame"—had already developed a highly advanced civilization on their own planet, and they taught the Lemurians how to achieve individual immortality and reincarnation. By the time of the seventh subrace, the Lemurians had mastered the basic arts of civilization and had begun to look human. The Lapps and the Australian Aborigines are among their descendants on earth today.

During the period of the sixth and seventh subraces Lemuria began to break up as various parts of the continent sank. But a peninsula of Lemuria that extended into the North Atlantic grew into Atlantis. Then the Fourth Root Race, the Atlantean, appeared on what was left of Lemuria. Some of its first subrace, the Rmoahals, moved to Atlantis. Others stayed behind and interbred with the Lemurians to produce a race of half-breeds, who looked like blue-skinned American Indians. The Rmoahals were black-skinned, and stood between 10 and 12 feet tall. The Rmoahals who settled in southern Atlantis waged continual war on the remaining Lemurians, but as time went on some Rmoahals moved to the north of Atlantis, where their skins became lighter and their stature shorter. Their descendants were the Cro-Magnons of Europe.

Next to arrive on the scene, according to Scott-Elliot, were the Tlavatlis. This second Atlantean subrace originated on an island off Atlantis that is now the site of Mexico. Gradually the human race was feeling its way toward self-government, and the appearance of the third subrace, the Toltecs, ushered in the golden age of Atlantis. The Toltecs enjoyed a superb culture for 100,000 years until they resorted to sorcery and phallic worship. There was a rebellion, and the followers of the "black arts" overthrew the emperor and replaced him with their own king. The Toltecs then degenerated, and were soon at war with the Turanians, the fourth subrace, who had meanwhile emerged on Atlantis. The Turanians were a brutal and ruthless people, and practiced complete sexual promiscuity in order to boost their population for warfare. Their direct descendants were the Aztecs.

During these wars—some 800,000 years ago—a great catastrophe caused most of Atlantis to disappear, reducing it to a relatively small island. At the same time, a number of islands began to grow in size on their way to becoming the continents we know today. Many of the surviving Turanians left for Asia where they evolved into the more civilized seventh subrace, the Mongolians. In the meantime, the fifth and sixth subraces, the Semites and the Akkadians, came into being on Atlantis. The Semites inhabited the northern region of Atlantis, which is now Scotland and Ireland, and were a quarrelsome people who constantly provoked fights with their neighbors, the peaceful Akkadians.

Right: a Lemurian, as described by occultist W. Scott-Elliot in his account of the continent. *The Lost Lemuria*. Like Madame Blavatsky, Scott-Elliot divided man into root races, and this "average, common-place" Lemurian belonged, so he wrote, to the fifth subrace of the third root race. He was a gigantic, ungainly being, between 12 and 15 feet tall, with long arms and legs permanently bent at elbow and knee, and huge hands and feet. His heels projected backward because, in the early stages of their evolution, Lemurians could walk backward as efficiently as forward—to aid them, they had a third eye in the back of their head. This creature's two primary eyes were set far apart, so that he could see sideways as well as forward, and lurked beneath a roll of flesh that took the place of a forehead. His whole face was curiously flattened, his skin dark, and his general aspect hideous—as was that of the huge reptile he led by a rope of twisted creeper. Lemurians, Scott-Elliot asserted, domesticated these sinister monsters and used them as companions in the hunt.

Another disaster 200,000 years ago split what was left of Atlantis into two islands—Ruta, ruled by surviving Toltec sorcerers, and Daitya, occupied by Semite sorcerers. The next phase in the destruction occurred 80,000 years ago when a further catastrophe submerged Daitya and made Ruta an even smaller island. It was the final sinking of Ruta—also called Poseidonis—in 9564 B.C. that inspired Plato's story. Before the disaster that destroyed Daitya, a selected band of Semites moved into Central Asia where they evolved into the Aryans, the Fifth Root Race, who include the modern Hindus and Europeans.

There was far more to Scott-Elliot's story than this complex account of racial evolution. He was able to list the great achievements of the Atlanteans, such as the domestication of leopard-like animals and the creation of the banana. Atlantean alchemists made huge quantities of precious metals. Atlantean scientists invented gas-bombs and aircraft propelled by jets of *vril*-force, a mentally directed, invisible force first dreamed up by a Victorian novelist. These aircraft, owned only by the rich, flew at 100 mph and had a ceiling of 1000 feet. They were even capable of vertical takeoff, and Scott-Elliot's description of this aeronautical feat is not too different from the "jump jet" technique used today.

Another detail-packed interpretation of the lost continents of Atlantis and Lemuria came from the pen of Rudolf Steiner, a

Below: Scott-Elliot's map of the continent of Lemuria "at its greatest extent." The map was based, he wrote, on a "broken terra-cotta model and a very badly preserved and crumpled map," amplified by occult memories of the period in earth's history the map represents. Scott-Elliot was reluctant to assign a precise date to his representations of Lemuria, but did state that the continent probably looked like this from the Permian into the Jurassic—that is, from approximately 280 million to 180 million years ago.

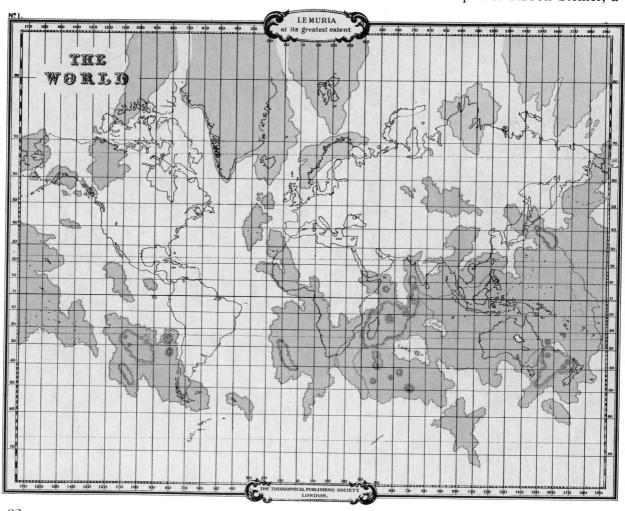

tall, dark-eyed Austrian who broke away from the Theosophists in 1907 to form his own Anthroposophical Society. Steiner's *Cosmic Memory: Atlantis and Lemuria*, published in 1923, is still in print through Rudolf Steiner Publications, the publishing enterprise that also prints other Atlantis classics such as the works of Donnelly and Le Plongeon. Steiner claimed to have derived his view of the lost continents from consultation of what he called the "Akasha Chronicle"—a spiritual record of the past available only to the initiated. Nevertheless, many of his ideas are obviously drawn from the work of Madame Blavatsky.

Steiner's Lemurians were feeble-minded, but they had enormous willpower by which they could lift heavy weights. Young Lemurians were taught to bear pain as an aid to developing this willpower. The Lemurians were endowed with souls, and they slowly developed the rudiments of speech. During their period as egg-laying hermaphrodites, the Lemurians made do with a single eye, but their vision improved along with their discovery of sex. According to Steiner, while their souls dominated their bodies, the Lemurians remained bisexual, but when the earth entered "a certain stage of its densification," the increasing density of matter forced a division of the sexes. The Lemurians were unenthusiastic about this change, and for a long time they regarded sexual intercourse as a sacred duty rather than a

Below: Scott-Elliot's second map of Lemuria, representing the continent at a later period in its history. The earth's landmasses were thus arranged, according to Scott-Elliot, through the Cretaceous period and into the Eocene—from some 136 million to some 60 million years ago. At that time, "great catastrophes" had begun the dismemberment of Lemuria, but its final destruction was still far off. The occultist never professed that these maps were perfectly accurate, but he thought in important details they were probably correct.

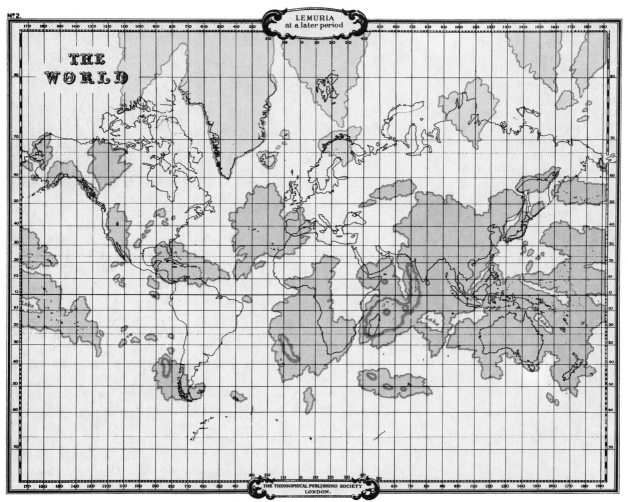

pleasure. The Lemurian women remained far more spiritual than their menfolk.

Steiner's Atlanteans, like the Lemurians, were unable to reason but they did possess good memories. They were educated in a way that enabled them to hold a vast store of images in their minds, and each problem was solved by remembering a precedent. When confronted with a novel situation, however, this system left them floundering. The Atlanteans had learned to control the "life force," which they were able to use to power their aircraft.

They had also discovered the magical power of certain words, which they used to heal the sick or to tame wild animals. They wove the branches of living trees to form their houses and cities. Toward the end of their racial history, when the Semites emerged, the Atlanteans had begun to lose their mastery of the life force and were allowing individualism to take over. However, the Semites developed reasoning and a conscience to take themselves a step further along the evolutionary scale, and their descendants, the Aryans, refined these qualities further still.

So what began as mere speculation in the minds of biologists looking for a land-bridge in the Indian Ocean has developed into a complex occult world picture centered on both Atlantis and Lemuria, which—depending on whose account is regarded as the most authoritative—might once have been joined together in a single massive continent that covered practically the entire Southern Hemisphere and stretched all the way into the North Atlantic.

It would be easy to dismiss Blavatsky, Scott-Elliot, and Steiner as cranks or fools, and their accounts as highly romanticized fiction with mass appeal. But would that be entirely fair? Do we know enough about man's spiritual and mental abilities to rule out the possibility of being able to step back in time? The field of parapsychology is a thriving if frustrating one, but there are certainly enough paranormal phenomena now under study for us to keep an open mind on the possibility of astral clairvoyance. Indeed some occultists have claimed that Plato himself might have used this method in compiling his Atlantis story.

It is intriguing to note that many early maps of the world showed a continental landmass in the Southern Hemisphere, long before anyone had ever mentioned Lemuria. The landmass, placed in the South Pacific, was named *Terra Australis Incognita*, "the great unknown southern continent," and no one was more surprised than the European explorers of the 16th and 17th centuries to discover little but sea in the vast Pacific Ocean. It has been argued that the belief in *Terra Australis Incognita* originated in the human desire for symmetry, which caused the Greeks to suppose that equal amounts of land were distributed, in symmetrical fashion, around the globe. Although this idea was modified by the voyages of Columbus and others, most people continued to think it reasonable that the same amount of land should be found below the equator as above it. The discovery of Australia in the 17th century failed to solve the problem, being too small and too barren a land to fulfill people's expectations about the great southern continent, and even when the great British explorer Captain James Cook had shown beyond doubt that no such continent existed in the South Pacific, some people clung to the idea that it must once have been there. Believers in this lost continent argue that our very desire for symmetry may be a manifestation of a deep, latent *knowing*— a collective subconscious memory of the land on which our ancestors evolved.

The problem with the occultists is that their stories go back so far in time. Scientists assure us that if such enormous changes in the earth's surface as the occultists describe did occur, they would have taken place long before man appeared on the planet. By the time our species was emerging the earth's crust was relatively peaceful, and has remained so ever since.

Probably most people today would prefer to fall in with an orthodox view of the earth backed by scientific evidence. But before we dismiss the occultists and their beliefs there is one important question that requires an answer: Why do the ancient myths and legends of practically every people tell of a tremendous catastrophe that once shook the earth? Perhaps the scientists are mistaken after all.

Atlantean Airships

The vast continent of Lemuria perished, according to Scott-Elliot, through volcanic action. But a northern peninsula in the Atlantic Ocean survived Lemuria's fiery destruction, and there the fourth root race of man evolved. This was the Atlantean race, and civilization first emerged in its home, the legendary Atlantis.

The civilization of Scott-Elliot's Atlantis sounds like a modern SF dream. Its scientific knowledge was in any case far in advance of that of the late 19th century, when Scott-Elliot wrote. He even credited the Atlanteans with the invention of airships, powered in their early days by life force or *vril*, but in later times by a "force not yet discovered by science." This mysterious fuel enabled the Atlantean upper classes—for whose sole use the airships were originally reserved—to travel at up to 100 miles an hour.

Atlantean airships were built first from wood, later from a metallic alloy, but in either case they appeared "seamless and perfectly smooth, and they shone in the dark as if coated with luminous paint." They were boat-shaped, with a ramming nose, and decked over to protect their passengers at speed. At first they carried only a few passengers; later, fighting airships holding 50 or 100 men were built.

Legends of Fire and Flood

The earth was at peace. A mild climate enveloped the planet and man had responded well to the beneficence of nature. He had learned to cultivate and harvest his crops. He had domesticated animals to help make his life easier. Various civilizations were beginning to blossom. Then a terrible and all-encompassing catastrophe shook the earth.

The sky lit up with a strange celestial display. Those who saw in this a portent of disaster fled for shelter. Those who watched and waited perished as the sky grew dark and a fearful rain fell upon the earth. In places the rain was red like blood. In others it was like

Right: a 19th-century artist's representation of the biblical story of the destruction of Sodom and Gomorrah. Such tales of a terrible devastation caused by volcanic eruption, fire, or flood are common to the mythologies of peoples throughout the world. Are they based on folk memories of an appalling holocaust by which the entire earth was once shaken? Or is each legend founded on a smaller, more localized event?

"A terrifying event of global proportion"

gravel or hailstones. And it brought down fire from the sky, too. Nothing escaped this global holocaust. Men and animals were engulfed. Forests were crushed. Even those who reached the caves were not safe. Darkness gripped the earth and tremendous quakes convulsed the planet. Mountains were thrown up to the heavens and continents were sucked beneath the seas as the stricken earth rolled and tilted. Hurricane winds lashed the planet's wretched surface and tidal waves swept across vast stretches of land. Fearful explosions shook the world as molten lava spewed out from the broken crust. A terrible heat hung over the planet and in places even the sea boiled.

Some, miraculously, lived through this horrific turmoil. After many long days of darkness the mantle of gloom was lifted from the earth and the survivors slowly began rebuilding their lives. A catastrophe of such proportions would account for the sinking of a huge continent such as Atlantis—but did such an event ever take place?

If it did, we might expect to find evidence of it in the myths, legends, and folklore of the people who survived. It is a remarkable fact that almost all races have a tradition, handed down through countless generations, of a catastrophe that nearly ended the world. Not only are these legends similar in essence, they are also frequently similar in detail, to such an extent that it is tempting to assume they all share a common origin: a terrifying event of global proportions.

The Babylonian *Epic of Gilgamesh*, which is around 4000 years old and records traditions of an even earlier age, tells of a dark cloud that rushed at the earth, leaving the land shriveled by the heat of the flames: "Desolation . . . stretched to heaven; all that was bright was turned into darkness. . . . Nor could a brother distinguish his brother. . . . Six days . . . the hurricane, deluge, and tempest continued sweeping the land . . . and all human life back to its clay was returned."

From ancient Hindu legend comes an account of the appearance in the sky of "a being shaped like a boar, white and exceedingly small; this being, in the space of an hour, grew to the size of an elephant of the largest size, and remained in the air." After some time the "boar" suddenly uttered "a sound like the loudest thunder, and the echo reverberated and shook all the quarters of the universe." This object then became a "dreadful spectacle," and "descended from the region of the air, and plunged head-foremost into the water. The whole body of water was convulsed by the motion, and began to rise in waves, while the guardian spirit of the sea, being terrified, began to tremble for his domain and cry for mercy."

Hesiod, a Greek poet of the 8th century B.C., writes of a legend involving the earth and the heavens. The story centers around a fiery, serpentlike creature, an aerial monster mightier than men and gods alike, that wreaks terrible havoc upon the earth: "Harshly then he thundered, and heavily and terribly the earth reechoed around; and the broad heaven above, and the sea and streams of ocean, and the abyss of earth. But beneath his immortal feet vast Olympus trembled, as the king uprose and earth groaned beneath. And the heat from both caught the dark-colored sea, both of the thunder and the lightning, and fire from

Left: Akkadian cylinder seal of the 3rd century B.C., depicting Zu, the bird-man, led for judgment before Ea, god of the deep. This reproduction is larger than the actual seal. One of the first flood myths belonged to the earliest civilizations of the Tigris-Euphrates valley. It told how Ea warned the earth of a disastrous inundation that was soon to come. Below: lightning flashing over the erupting volcano of Surtsey in 1963. The horror of volcanic eruptions helped create myths of a catastrophic end to the world.

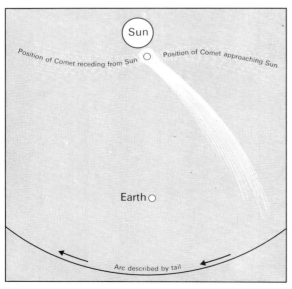

Above: *The Seventh Plague of Egypt*, a 19th-century painting of one of the terrible vengeances that, according to the Bible, God wreaked upon the enemies of the Jews. The Bible tells how Moses "stretched forth his rod toward heaven: and the Lord sent thunder and hail, and fire ran along the ground. . . ." In the view of Russo-Israeli cosmologist Immanuel Velikovsky, this archetypal catastrophe was part of a series of natural disasters caused by a comet nearly colliding with the earth.

Left: like Velikovsky, Ignatius Donnelly believed that a series of terrible catastrophes had once befallen the earth, caused when it passed through the tail of a comet, narrowly missing a collision.

Right: the Fenris wolf devours the god Odin, a scene from the Norse legend *Ragnarok*. Donnelly mistranslated Ragnarok as "rain of dust" and used the word as title of his book on the comet theory.

the monster, the heat arising from the thunderstorm, winds, and burning lightning. And all earth, and heaven, and sea were boiling. . . ."

From Iceland we have further evidence of a global catastrophe in the *Poetic Edda*, a collection of ancient Scandinavian legendary poems of unknown antiquity:

"Mountains dash together,
Heroes go the way to Hel,
and heaven is rent in twain. . . .
The sun grows dark,
The earth sinks into the sea,
The bright stars from heaven vanish;
Fire rages,
Heat blazes,
And high flames play
'Gainst heaven itself."

The legends of the Cashinaua, the aborigines of western Brazil, tell of the time when "The lightnings flashed and the thunders roared terribly and all were afraid. Then the heaven burst and the fragments fell down and killed everything and everybody. Heaven and earth changed places. Nothing that had life was left upon the earth."

In North America, the Choctaw Indians of Oklahoma have a tradition about the time when "The earth was plunged in darkness for a long time." A bright light eventually appeared in the north, "but it was mountain-high waves, rapidly coming nearer."

The Samoan aborigines of the South Pacific have a legend that says: "Then arose smell . . . the smell became smoke, which again became clouds. . . . The sea too arose, and in a stupendous catastrophe of nature the land sank into the sea. . . . The new earth (the Samoan islands) arose out of the womb of the last earth."

The Bible, too, contains numerous passages that refer to terrible conflagrations. Psalms 18:7–15 is one example: "Then the earth shook and trembled; the foundations also of the hills moved and were shaken. . . . The Lord also thundered in the heavens, and the Highest gave his voice; hail stones and coals of fire. . . . Then the channels of waters were seen, and the foundations of the world were discovered. . . ."

These are but a few of the vast number of legends dealing with great cosmic events and cataclysmic destruction on the face of the earth. The ancient records of Egypt, India, and China, the mythology of Greece and Rome, the legends of the Mayas and the Aztecs, the biblical accounts, and those of Norway, Finland, Persia, and Babylon, all tell the same story. So, too, do the people of widely separated countries, such as the Celts of Britain and the Maoris of New Zealand.

What on earth, or in heaven, could have caused such seemingly worldwide catastrophe? The accounts quoted above are taken from two masterly works on the subject, both of which offer the same explanation. One is Ignatius Donnelly's *Ragnarok: The Age of Fire and Gravel*, published in 1883, whose title is drawn from the legend of *Ragnarok* (wrongly translated as "the darkness of the gods" and "the rain of dust") contained in the Scandinavian *Poetic Edda*. The other is *Worlds in Collision*, which appeared in 1950, and is the most famous of several books by Immanuel Velikovsky, a Russo-Israeli physician whose theories have made him as controversial a character as Donnelly before him. Both men suggest that a comet which came into close proximity with the earth caused the terrible events remembered by the ancient peoples of the world. They agree on many points of evidence, such as the myths and legends, and the sinking of Atlantis features in both works. But they take different stands in their search for scientific proof of their theories.

Donnelly devotes a large part of his book to a discussion of the drift, or *till*—a vast deposit of sand, gravel, and clay that lies above the stratified rocks of the earth's surface. The origin of the till puzzled many geologists, and Donnelly's explanation was that it had rained down from the heavens as the earth passed through a comet's tail. He argued that the comet's tail would have been moving at close to the speed of light when the earth passed through it, so only half the planet would have been covered by the till, and he sought to produce evidence to confirm his theory.

Velikovsky, though agreeing that a close earth-comet encounter lay behind the ancient catastrophe legends, has no use for the till theory—which was a foundation stone of Donnelly's treatise—and he observes: "Donnelly . . . tried in his book *Ragnarok* to explain the presence of till and gravel on the rock substratum in America and Europe by hypothesizing an encounter with a comet, which rained till on the terrestrial hemisphere facing it at that moment. . . . His assumption that there is till only in one half of the earth is arbitrary and wrong."

Neither Donnelly nor Velikovsky was the first to argue that a comet had caused havoc on this planet. The English scientist William Whiston, who succeeded Sir Isaac Newton at Cambridge, wrote a book in 1696, *New Theory of the Earth*, which attempted to prove that a comet caused the biblical Flood. There was also a belief, at the time of Aristotle, in the 4th century B.C., that a comet had joined the solar system as a planet.

But Velikovsky has pieced together a far more startling picture of cosmic activity. It began, he believes, when a planetary collision caused Jupiter to eject a comet, which went into an eccentric orbit. This brought it close to the earth in about 1500 B.C., causing global catastrophes. The comet returned 52 years later and did further damage to the earth. Its approaches even caused the planet to stop and then rotate in the opposite direction, changing the position of the poles and altering the earth's orbit. The hydrocarbon gases of the comet's tail showered down on the earth in a rain of gravel and fire that formed the petroleum deposits we now use to power our automobiles and airplanes.

The comet, having left much of its tail behind, then had a close encounter with Mars, causing that planet to leave its orbit and, in turn, to come dangerously close to the earth in the 8th and 7th centuries B.C. Meanwhile the comet joined the solar system as a planet—the one we now call Venus.

When this theory was first published, in 1950, it caused a sensation. Since then Velikovsky has become something of a cult figure, particularly among young people, though the

Above: Immanuel Velikovsky. In 1950 Velikovsky published his controversial theory of planetary encounters in *Worlds in Collision*, and set people speculating on the evolution of the universe.

Right: the planet Venus. Velikovsky believes that Venus began its life between 4000 and 5000 years ago as a vast comet, which caused havoc in the universe before taking its own planetary place. It was a near collision between the comet Venus and the earth that caused the catastrophic natural disasters recorded in legends throughout the world.

Left: the beautifully colored comet Humason, which appeared in the night skies in 1961. If Immanuel Velikovsky's theory of cosmic evolution is correct, the planet Venus once looked like this as it sped toward the earth, bringing disaster in its train.

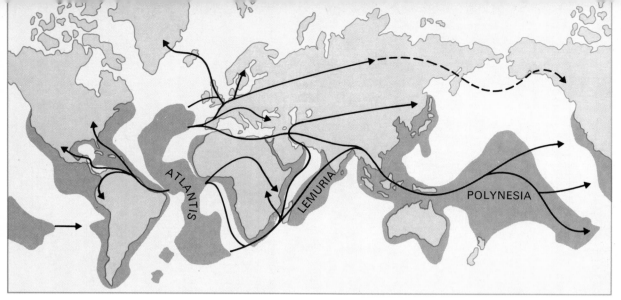

scientific community has largely dismissed his ideas as nonsense.

L. Sprague de Camp probably expresses the opinion of most orthodox scientists and scholars in his succinct and damning appraisal of Velikovsky's "mad" theory. He writes in *Lost Continents*: "Despite the impressive build-up . . . Velikovsky neither establishes a case nor accounts for the success of the Copernicus-Newton-Einstein picture of the cosmos which he undertook to supersede. Some of his mythological references are wrong (for instance he uses the Brasseur 'translation' of the *Troano Codex*); the rest merely demonstrate once again that the corpus of recorded myth is so vast that you can find mythological allusions to back up any cosmological speculation you please. The Babylonians left clear records of observations of Venus 5000 years ago, behaving just as it does now. . . . Moreover, the theory is ridiculous from the point of view of physics and mechanics. Comets are not planets and do not evolve into planets; instead they are loose aggregations of meteors with total masses less than a millionth that of the earth. Such a mass—about that of an ordinary mountain—could perhaps devastate several counties or a small state if struck, but could not appreciably affect the earth's orbit, rotation, inclination, or other components of movement. . . . And the gas of which the comet's tail is composed is so attenuated that if the tail of a good-sized comet were compressed to the density of iron, I could put the whole thing in my briefcase!"

So that disposes of Velikovsky—or does it? Seven years after his book was published, man made his first tentative steps into space. Since then earthlings have landed on the moon, and space vehicles have probed our nearest planetary neighbors. So far, these explorations appear to have confirmed some of Velikovsky's predictions about our planetary system. He had stated that, because Venus is a newcomer to the system, it is still giving off heat. This was thought to be nonsense at the time, and the consensus of astronomical opinion was that the surface temperature of Venus was around 65°F. Radio astronomy and the arrival of space vehicles in the vicinity of the planet have proved Velikovsky right. Mariner II, when it passed Venus in December 1962, detected a temperature of over 800°F, and subsequent in-

vestigations have revealed a temperature of approximately 990°F.

The results of the Mariner probe—the first to provide reliable information about the planet—showed that, just as Velikovsky had maintained, Venus is enclosed in an envelope of hydrocarbon gases and dust. It was also revealed that Venus rotated retrogradely, a sign that either it had been disturbed or it had evolved in a different way from other planets. A Russian probe that soft-landed on the planet in October 1975 was able to relay information for 53 minutes before the extremely high pressure of the atmosphere caused it to stop transmitting. But it was enough for the Russian scientists to declare that Venus is a young planet, and still "alive."

Interviewed about these findings by a British newspaper, Velikovsky commented that they confirmed his theory. His book contained many other predictions about Mars, Jupiter, the earth, and the moon. "And about 30 of them have since been proved right," he claimed. If subsequent probes confirm other details of his theory, it would not be the first time that science has had to change its thinking about the history of the earth and its partners in the solar system.

Velikovsky weaves the destruction of Atlantis into his theory by suggesting that the continent sank as a result of the first approach of the Venus comet, though in order to make this idea fit his scheme he has to alter Plato's dating of the Atlantis catastrophe. There is one zero too many in Plato's date, says Velikovsky. Atlantis sank not 9000 years before Solon's trip to Egypt, but 900 years before Solon—in about 1500 B.C.

The idea that a comet destroyed Atlantis was not a new one. It had previously been put forward in 1785 by the Italian scholar Gian Rinaldo Carli—although he dated the catastrophe at 4000 B.C.—and was taken up again in the 1920s by a German writer called Karl Georg Zschaetzch, whose main aim was to prove the racial superiority of the Aryans by providing them with a pedigree that went all the way back to Atlantis.

Another theory to account for the Atlantis catastrophe came from Hanns Hörbiger, an Austrian inventor and engineer. Hörbiger maintained that the universe is filled with "cosmic building stuff," consisting of hot metallic stars and "cosmic ice." The collision between a hot star and a block of cosmic ice generates a tremendous explosion, throwing pieces of star material and ice particles into space. These bodies spiral inward toward the sun, causing another explosion, which covers the nearest planets with a thick coating of ice. Hörbiger believed the Milky Way to consist of ice particles, and maintained that Venus and Mercury were sheathed in ice, as was the moon. According to Hörbiger's theory, the earth had possessed several moons before the present one. Each of these moons caused violent earthquakes and floods on the earth at the time of its capture by our planet, and finally shattered, showering its fragments onto the earth's surface. These events gave rise to the catastrophe myths, and it was the capture of our present moon that caused both Atlantis and Lemuria to sink. Hörbiger predicted that the eventual breakup and fall of our present moon would probably wipe out life on earth.

Hörbiger's theory, published in 1913, attracted millions of

followers, and made him as much of a cult figure as Velikovsky is today. But whereas space exploration and our increased knowledge of the universe have disproved most of Hörbiger's assertions, many of Velikovsky's ideas are still living up to the expectations of his followers, who foresee them becoming the accepted scientific thinking of a future era. Unless and until that day comes, however, we need to examine the catastrophe legends and the theories of lost continents in the light of current scientific belief. The picture then becomes far less promising.

Orthodox scientists dismiss the idea of a global catastrophe of the kind described by Velikovsky and others. How, then, do they explain the legends? The answer is that, universal though the disaster legends may seem, they are descriptions of separate

Left: *The Deluge*, a 19th-century depiction of the great flood with which, according to the Bible, God punished the world. So vast was the cataclysm that, apart from those warned by God, every living thing perished. Today orthodox scholars believe that the flood described in the Bible was based on an inundation that swamped the Euphrates Valley some 7000 years ago. To those ancient peoples it must have seemed as though the entire world had been drowned. Below: Noah's ark rides the floodwaters, watched over by God. Noah, warned by God of the approaching flood, saved his family and male and female representatives of every animal species in his ark.

events that occurred at different times and were fairly localized. They concern tremendous earthquakes, great volcanic eruptions, massive flooding of river valleys, and inundation of areas below sea level. These events, spanning many centuries and not linked in any way, gave rise to the legends, which were doubtless exaggerated as they were handed down from one generation to the next.

Take Noah's flood, for example. According to the Bible, this great deluge drowned every living thing on earth—apart from the few survivors in the ark. It is now considered likely that this story was based on a real flood that submerged something like 40,000 square miles of the Euphrates Valley some time between 5400 and 4200 B.C. China and the lowlands of Bengal have seen

冨嶽三十六景／神奈川沖浪裏

Above: Japanese artist Hokusai's print of a tidal wave, another of the natural disasters that can devastate the earth. A tidal wave breaking on the shore causes immense damage and many deaths. It can be set off by an earthquake or volcanic eruption, and the combination of earth tremor, fire, and flood appears in many myths about the end of the world. **Right:** a tidal wave engulfing a British steamship off the West Indies in 1867. The widespread incidence of such disasters may account for their presence in the myths of so many different races.

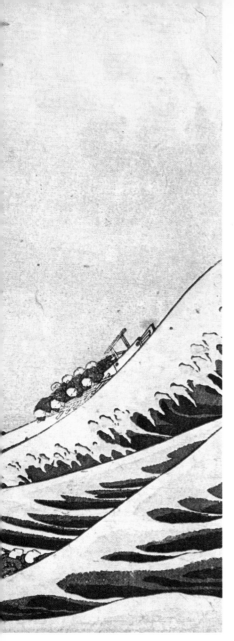

similar great floods, and these, too, could have given rise to deluge legends. Many geologists believe that the Mediterranean was once a fertile valley below sea level, which was flooded long ago by the Atlantic in one terrible rush. The flooding of the former Zuider Zee (now IJssel Lake) in the Netherlands is a more recent example of this kind of catastrophe. A storm in 1282 broke the natural dykes that protected this area of sub-sea-level land, and let in the North Sea, which submerged it in a single day.

In this century alone there have been a number of earthquakes that have taken in excess of 100,000 lives, and there are records of even more disastrous quakes in the past. The Chinese earthquake of 1556 is said to have killed 830,000 people. It would be surprising if similar quakes in ancient times did *not* give rise to catastrophe legends. To those living in the affected areas it must certainly have seemed as if the whole world were coming to an end.

An earthquake beneath the sea may cause a tidal wave. In mid-ocean the gentle slopes of a tidal wave may go undetected, but as the wave approaches and meets the shore it surges up into a massive, sometimes skyscraper-high, wall of water. In 1737, a 210-foot tidal wave was recorded in Kamchatka (now part of the eastern Soviet Union), and many others have been reported between 50 and 100 feet tall. Volcanic eruptions, in addition to wreaking their own havoc, may also set up tidal waves. The Krakatoa eruption of 1883 caused a huge wave that drowned 36,380 people living on the shores of the nearby Indonesian islands.

So, our history is rich in natural disasters that have taken a tremendous toll of human life—as they still do—and that may well have given rise to the legends. But could any of these pestilences account for the sinking of a great continent such as Atlantis? Most scientists think it extremely unlikely. An earthquake might have destroyed part of the island continent, or caused landslides around its shores, but the total area devastated by even a violent earthquake is relatively limited, and a quake that would have destroyed a huge landmass is unheard-of. Had Atlantis been an island with a very low profile it might have been at least partly submerged by flooding, but Plato describes Atlantis as a mountainous country. A tidal wave might have washed over Atlantis, but it would not have washed it away. And a volcanic eruption could have blown part of the continent into the ocean, but if Atlantis had been anywhere near the size claimed by Plato much would still be towering above the sea. In the scientists' view even a whole series of massive earthquakes, volcanic eruptions, and flooding would take many thousands of years to sink an island of anything approaching continental size— and a low, flat island at that.

The only other possibility would seem to be that the earth's crust is capable of opening up and swallowing areas of land. Small islands have been submerged in living memory, and others have suddenly appeared. Could the same forces have been responsible for wiping Atlantis from the face of our planet? To answer this question we need to look at present opinion on the way the world has developed, and at the processes by which continents take shape.

According to current geological theory, the earth is encased in a crust of rock that becomes hotter and hotter as we go down toward the center of the planet. Some 50 to 100 miles beneath the surface the rock has become white-hot. From that point down the earth consists of a hot, glasslike substance called *magma*, which surrounds the nickel-iron core of the earth, a sphere about 4000 miles in diameter. The cool exterior rocks consist in general of two types: dense, heavy, magnesium-bearing rocks, called *sima*, which form most of the ocean floors, and light, aluminum-bearing rocks, called *sial*, which form most of the land areas. Geologists see the continents as beds of sial "floating" on a crust of sima. The continental blocks descend deeply into the sima, showing a comparatively small amount above the surface, just as icebergs do in water.

Over a century ago, it became apparent to some geologists that the face of our globe has not always been as it now appears. The evidence for this assumption was the same that led many biologists of the time to consider the possibility of a lost continent: namely, the existence of fossils of similar fauna and flora on continents thousands of miles apart.

Geologists who accepted fossil evidence of ancient land connections between the continents put forward the idea of a former gigantic landmass, which they called Gondwanaland, comprising present-day South America, Africa, India, Australia, and Antarctica. A second landmass, consisting of North America and Europe, was also suggested and given the name Laurasia. However, the proponents of this theory were unable to offer any convincing evidence as to how these two supercontinents might have broken up, and their idea attracted little support among fellow scientists.

Nevertheless, in the early years of the 20th century, a number of scientists began thinking along similar lines, and in 1915 the German astronomer, geophysicist, and meteorologist Alfred Wegener published the modern theory of continental drift. Wegener argued that if the continents float like icebergs on the sima crust, why should they not also drift like icebergs across the face of the earth? He suggested that all the modern continents were once joined in a single giant landmass. They have since drifted apart, and the drift is continuing; millions of years from now, the face of our planet will look very different from the way it does today.

Philippine

Indian

Wegener's theory has rocked the geological establishment, and its revolutionary effect on the geological sciences has been compared to the effect of Darwin's theory of evolution on the biological sciences a century ago. But for several decades after its publication the majority of scientists continued to reject the idea of continental drift, mainly because they found it hard to envisage forces strong enough to move the continents around. (After all, even the smallest continent, Australia, weighs around 500 million million million kilograms.) In due course, however, a plausible explanation—involving convection currents driven by radioactive heat from within the earth—was put forward to account for the continental movements, and a mass of impressive evidence began piling up in support of Wegener's theory, so that most scientists now accept the reality of continental drift.

In the late 1960s computers were used to show how the

Left: Alfred Wegener, German geophysicist who proposed the theory of continental drift. According to this theory, the continents we know today were once joined in a single landmass. When this broke up, the many pieces "drifted" to their present positions on the earth's surface. Below: world map overprinted with lines representing the edges of the largest of the 19 "plates" that make up the earth's crust. Geological activity takes place mainly on the joins between the plates and Atlantists believe that during such movement Atlantis could have sunk into the earth.

continental jigsaw pieces might fit together to form the original gigantic landmass. This was not an easy task, because the shape of the continents has altered over the ages. Some minor parts of the jigsaw are missing, some have been added, and the true edges of the continents generally lie far below sea level and have not yet been plotted in detail. Nevertheless, the computer pictures showed an extremely good fit between South America and the western coast of Africa, and between Antarctica, Australia, and India. The fit of these last three continents against south and eastern Africa was less satisfactory, and some adjustment was needed to improve the fit across the North Atlantic, linking Britain and the rest of Europe with North America.

In their book *Continental Drift*, leading British geophysicist D. P. Tarling and his technical journalist wife M. P. Tarling write: "By studying the size and composition of particles in old sedimentary rocks it is possible to work out the direction and

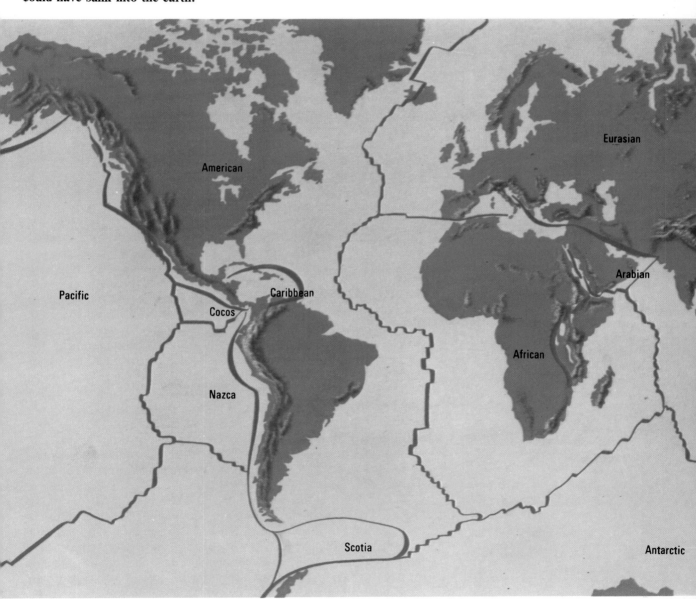

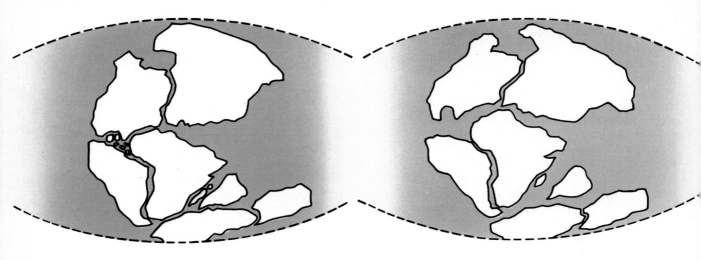

The earth 200 million years ago

The earth 135 million years ago

Above: how the continental drift theory positions the continents on the earth's crust at various epochs. The landmasses were originally joined together in one vast supercontinent, Pangaea. Some 180 million years ago, this began to split into two smaller but still huge landmasses, Laurasia in the north and Gondwana land in the south, These too broke up, and by 65 million years ago the shapes and positions of the continents began to resemble those we know today. The evidence of continental drift and of the geological composition of the earth's crust seems to rule out the possibility that continents other than ours ever existed. But does it? Might fresh geological evidence start the search again?

type of land from which they were derived. In Britain, we find that the source of many Caledonian Mountain sediments was a very extensive landmass which must have lain to the north and west where there is now the deep Atlantic Ocean. In North America, the sources of many Appalachian rocks lay to the south and east. To explain this before the acceptance of continental drift, geologists supposed that a continent 'Atlantis,' must have occupied the present position of the Atlantic. This continent was thought to have sunk beneath the Atlantic waves. [But] there can be no question of the existence of a sunken continent in the Atlantic. By reconstructing the jigsaw we not only fit together the Caledonian Mountain chain, but also explain the sources of the sediments which formed it."

Most scientists agree that as we push the continents back to their original places, we effectively squeeze Atlantis off the map. So, could Atlantis have been North America, which, having drifted away, was thought to have been submerged in the Atlantic? No. The continents are moving apart at the rate of between one and six inches a year—hardly enough to give rise to Plato's account of the submergence of Atlantis in a day and a night. What is more, the original landmass is thought to have broken up before the Mesozoic Era, some 200 million years ago, and the continents probably reached approximately their present positions by the beginning of the Cenozoic era, around 70 million years ago—long before man appeared on the face of the earth.

Could Atlantis have been in the Pacific, where Mu was said to have sunk, or in the Indian Ocean, where the early Lemuria enthusiasts placed yet another lost continent? Our present knowledge of the earth seems to rule out these possibilities, too. Bearing in mind the geologists' belief that the ocean floors are mostly formed of sima and the landmasses of sial, a sunken continent should be easy to detect because its rocks would be

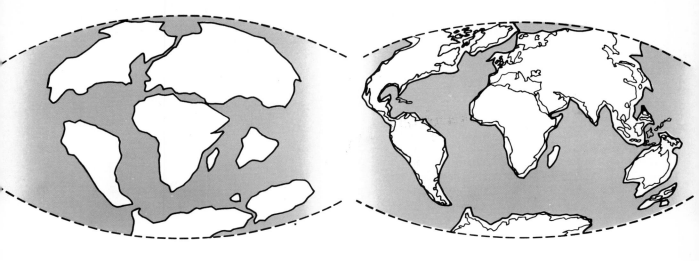

The earth 65 million years ago   The earth's continents today

different from surrounding rocks in the deep ocean. However, geological investigation has so far revealed that the greatest areas of deep sima are in the Central Pacific, the southern Indian Ocean, and the Arctic Ocean, making these the least likely sites on earth for a vanished continent.

Not surprisingly, believers in Atlantis hotly contest the findings of modern science that seek to dismiss the existence of the lost continent. In considering the theory of continental drift they point to gaps and seeming misfits in the linking of continents across the Atlantic that might still leave room for Atlantis. Nor are they impressed by the failure of oceanographers to find evidence of a sunken civilization beneath the Atlantic. In his book *The Mystery of Atlantis*, Charles Berlitz points out that even the underwater cities of the Mediterranean have been discovered only comparatively recently and in relatively shallow water. How much more difficult, then, to discover the ruins of Atlantis beneath the far larger Atlantic, where they would be smothered by sedimentation and mud accumulated over thousands of years.

If a once-derided theory such as continental drift can eventually earn the backing of the respectable scientific community, the Atlantists argue, might not other theories, now regarded as nonsensical, one day gain the same acceptance? Perhaps man existed long before the scientists' estimates. Perhaps there was some extraordinary global catastrophe of a nature quite outside the bounds of cautious scientific conjecture. Perhaps Atlantis did exist after all.

Recent scientific findings and theories may have helped modern man put the search for Atlantis into perspective, but they have not proved the lost continent to be a myth. In fact, some investigators among scientists themselves believe they have now discovered the true site of Atlantis, far away from the huge ocean so long regarded as its resting place.

7

Has Atlantis Been Found?

Until the beginning of this century most historians regarded the island of Crete as an unimportant place. True, the ancient Greeks had numerous stories and legends about this mountainous island at the southern end of the Aegean Sea. They looked upon Crete as the one-time home of a mighty seafaring people ruled by King Minos, the son of Zeus and the mortal maiden Europa. Legend had it that a bronze robot, with a man's body and a bull's head, patrolled Crete's rocky coastline, keeping invaders at bay by hurling boulders at them. There, too, was the labyrinth in which King Minos imprisoned the Minotaur, the monstrous bull-man who

Right: sunset over the Kameni Islands, photographed from Thera. In the Bronze Age, Thera was the home of a prosperous civilization closely linked with that of Minoan Crete. Then, in about 1500 B.C., its smouldering volcano erupted, smothering the island with pumice and ash and causing its central portion to sink into the sea. Today, Thera is the largest of three islands that mark the perimeter of the submerged crater or *caldera* of the volcano. In the center of the caldera rise the Kameni Islands, still-smouldering volcanic cones. Archaeologists excavating on Crete and Thera have found similarities between their civilizations and that of Atlantis as described by Plato. Some are convinced that the Greek philosopher based his fabulous continent on old memories of Thera and Crete.

116

"The palace walls were resplendent with paintings"

annually devoured seven Greek youths and seven Greek maidens, and who was finally slain by the Greek hero Theseus.

To most historians these stories were nothing more than colorful myths. It took the excavations of British archaeologist Sir Arthur Evans to prove that the legends were founded on fact. In 1900, Evans began uncovering astonishingly beautiful and sophisticated buildings on the island of Crete. His discoveries, together with subsequent finds, revealed that a highly advanced civilization had existed on Crete 4500 years ago. Evans gave this civilization the name Minoan for the legendary King Minos.

Minoans ruled the Aegean while the Greeks were still barbarians. Not only traders, but also colonizers, they were able to extract tribute from less advanced peoples such as the Greeks, and were known as far away as northern and western Europe, as well as in Egypt and the eastern Mediterranean, for their seagoing power, their wealth, and their gracious style of living.

Knossos, near modern Heraklion, about three miles from the coast of northern Crete, was the Minoan capital, and in 2500 B.C. it probably housed about 100,000 people. The palace of Knossos, home of the king and queen and a center of Minoan government, was a magnificent complex of buildings covering six acres. The elaborate plan of its rooms, halls, and courts, with their stately porticoes, shrines, tapered columns, and terraces, built on many different levels and linked by stairways and twisting passages, could well have given rise to Greek tales of a labyrinth on the island of Crete. The palace's huge storerooms contained supplies of grain, wine, and oil. Some jars kept there were able to hold up to 79,000 gallons of olive oil. The palace was also a religious and artistic center, with homes for priests and priestesses and workshops for artists and craftsmen, who held a highly respected place in Minoan society. The palace walls were resplendent with brilliantly colored paintings of birds, beasts, flowers, and young men and women in fashionable dress.

Frescoes and pottery found in Knossos and elsewhere express the Minoans' love of bright colors and swirling shapes, their keen observation of nature, and their zest for living. Their paintings show dancing and feasting, celebrations and sport, plants and animals, rather than battles or sieges—and everywhere their regard for the bull is apparent. Murals and vases show young, unarmed Minoans fearlessly leaping over the back of a bull, and a particularly striking ritual vessel is made in the form of a bull's head with golden horns. Other magnificent treasures, including beautifully wrought gold jewelry, and tools and ornaments inlaid with gold and ivory, testify to the reality of the Minoans' legendary wealth.

Not only did the Minoans live in beautiful surroundings but they enjoyed comforts unmatched until modern times. The palace in Knossos had flushing toilets, running water, and a well-planned drainage system for rainwater and sewage. Its rooms were ingeniously lit by windows opening onto light wells—possibly the earliest example of indirect lighting. The palace was surrounded by a town of 22 acres, containing the houses of sea captains, merchants, and shipowners, and a paved road with drains on either side ran all the way from Knossos to the south coast. Near the southern shore of Crete stood another magnifi-

Above: part of the main staircase of the Palace of Knossos in Crete. In 1900, British archaeologist Arthur Evans began excavations at Knossos that revealed Crete as the home of one of the most striking civilizations of the ancient world. Evans called the civilization Minoan, after the legendary King Minos of Crete. Left: the head of a Minoan woman, a fragment of a fresco found at Knossos. The Minoan civilization seems to have laid great emphasis on beauty and on pleasure—unlike contemporary civilizations, but like that of the Atlantis Plato described. Right: the "Harvester Vase." Agriculture flourished in Crete, as in Plato's Atlantis.

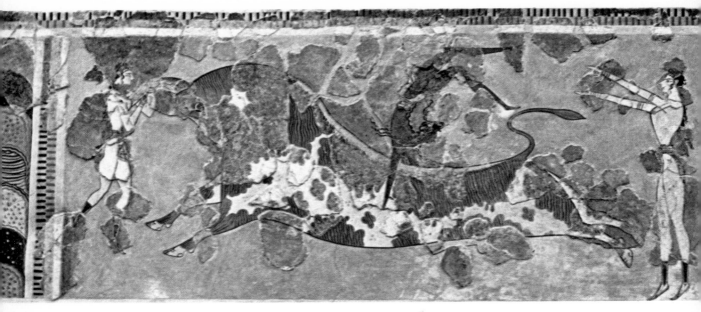

Above: the bull leap, a fresco from the Palace of Knossos depicting the dangerous but exhilarating bull games that the Minoans loved. As the excavations at Knossos progressed, it became clear that the bull was of immense importance to the life and mythology of Minoan Crete—and that it could provide some evidence to identify Crete with Atlantis. The bull, and bull ceremonies, featured largely in the life of Plato's Atlantis too.

cent city called Phaistos, and about 100 smaller cities or towns were scattered across the island. Archaeological studies have established that the civilization of Crete flourished for about 2000 years, but that it suffered an abrupt collapse around 1500 to 1400 B.C.

Here, for the first time, was evidence that a people very similar to the Atlanteans described by Plato had once existed. It was not long before some scholars were asking if a memory of this great culture had given rise to the Atlantis legend. Both Atlantis and Crete were island kingdoms and great sea powers, and both had suffered a sudden downfall. There seemed to be links, too, between the bull ceremonies depicted in Minoan art and the ritual hunting of the bull said to have taken place on Atlantis.

The first man to point out the similarities between Plato's Atlantis and the Minoan civilization was K. T. Frost, professor of classical history at Queen's University, Belfast. In 1909 Frost wrote in *The Times* of London about the need to reconsider the whole scheme of Mediterranean history as a result of the excavations on Crete, adding: "The whole description of Atlantis which is given in the *Timaeus* and the *Critias* has features so thoroughly Minoan that even Plato could not have invented so many unsuspected facts."

Recalling Plato's story, Frost went on to observe: "The great harbor, for example, with its shipping and its merchants coming from all parts, the elaborate bathrooms, the stadium, and the solemn sacrifice of a bull are all thoroughly, though not exclusively, Minoan; but when we read how the bull is hunted 'in the temple of Poseidon without weapons but with staves and nooses' we have an unmistakable description of the bull-ring at Knossos, the very thing which struck foreigners most and which gave rise to the legend of the Minotaur. Plato's words exactly describe the scenes on the famous Vapheio cups which certainly represent catching wild bulls for the Minoan bull-fight which, as we know from the palace itself, differed from all others which the world has seen in exactly the point which Plato emphasizes—namely that no weapons were used."

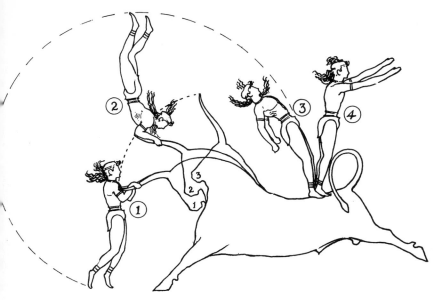

Left: the stages in the bull leap, reconstructed from the fresco opposite for Arthur Evans's book, *The Palace of Minos at Knossos*. First, the acrobat seized the bull by the tips of its horns (1), then somersaulting into the air over the animal's head (2). He would have gained impetus for his leap when the bull raised its head to toss him. Loosing the horns, he landed on his feet on the bull's back (3), then jumped or somersaulted to the comparative safety of the ground (4). It appears from paintings and sculptures discovered at Knossos that such games really took place in Crete—yet, as Evans wrote, they "transcend the power and skill of mortal man."

But Crete is not in the Atlantic. It is nowhere near the size of the great island continent described by Plato. And it has not disappeared beneath the waves. Frost argued that the sudden eclipse of Minoan power was probably caused by invasions from the Greek mainland—a point of view shared by most of his fellow scholars—but few were prepared to accept his suggestion that the loss of contact with their Minoan trading partners had led the Egyptians to believe that Crete had sunk beneath the sea. Frost's theory was therefore dismissed by the academic world, and after his death in World War I his ideas were forgotten.

Thirty years after the publication of Frost's theory, however,

Below: reconstruction of the Palace of Knossos. It covered a vast area and—built as it was on different levels linked by twisting passages and stairs—could have given rise to the myth of the Cretan labyrinth where the bull monster, the Minotaur, dwelt. Plato tells of a bull hunt in the Temple of Poseidon in Atlantis, yet another example of remarkable coincidence between myth and fact.

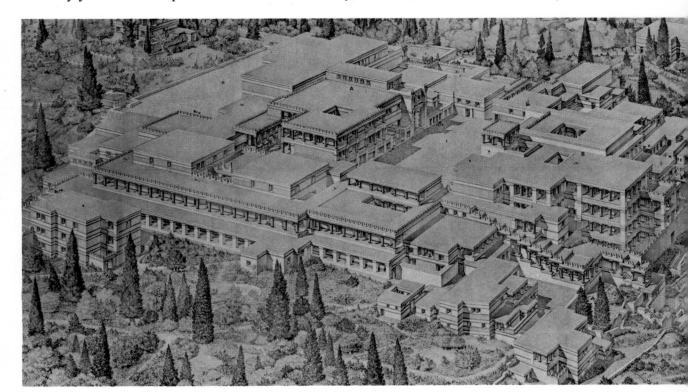

Professor Spyridon Marinatos, later Director-General of the Greek Archaeological Service, put forward new evidence that appeared to strengthen Frost's case. In an article entitled "The Volcanic Destruction of Minoan Crete," published in the British journal *Antiquity* in 1939, Marinatos told how, during his excavations in Amnisos, the site of an ancient harbor close to Knossos, he had discovered a pit full of pumice stone. He also found evidence that a vast mass of water had washed over the site, dragging large objects out of place. Marinatos became convinced that Crete's downfall was due not to foreign invaders, as most scholars still assumed, but to a tremendously violent natural catastrophe. He was also able to point an accusing finger at the probable source of this devastation: a small volcanic island named Thera, just 75 miles north of Crete, and the most southerly island in the archipelago of the Cyclades.

Thera has been given a number of names. Some people today know it as Santorini, a name derived from Saint Irene, the patron saint of the island. In the past, it has been called Kallistē ("the very beautiful island") and Strongulē ("the circular island").

Left: the strangely colored cliffs that delineate the submerged caldera of the Thera volcano. Some of the rocks are black, some red, and some white—the three colors Plato specifically names in his description of the stone used in the building of Atlantis. Below: Minoan ships spread the influence of their civilization far beyond Crete and the islands. On this map of Crete, Greece, and the Aegean, stars represent Minoan settlements, arrows trade routes.

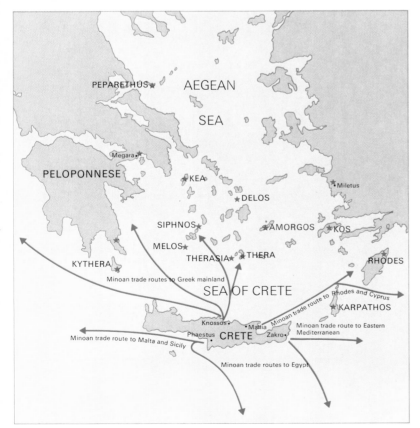

The truth about the Fall of Atlantis?

"But afterward there occurred violent earthquakes and floods; and in a single day and night of destruction...the island of Atlantis...disappeared into the depths of the sea." So wrote Plato. But how did Atlantis really fall?

About 3500 years ago, violent earthquakes shook the Aegean. The volcano of Thera erupted, belching out great clouds of ash that buried the land on which it fell. Huge masses of pumice were thrown forth, rendering the sea "impassable and impenetrable," and white-hot lava fragments were hurled into the air.

The violence of the explosions caused catastrophic aerial vibrations that reverberated through the Aegean, shaking and destroying buildings. The entire central portion of Thera collapsed, setting up tsunamis that drowned all in their path.

Only 75 miles from Thera lay Crete. Between the two islands there was nothing to break the force of the explosion; no land to stem the first destructive fury of the tsunamis; no protection from the falling snow of lava and ash. It seems indisputable that it was the Thera eruption that ended Minoan power in the Mediterranean. Might the land it destroyed have been Atlantis? As yet, we cannot be sure.

Although these two names preserve a memory of how the island used to look, neither description is appropriate today. Once a circular island, about 11 miles across, covered by cone-shaped peaks, with woods and good vegetation, Thera now consists of three fragments of its former glory. The largest is a crescent-shaped island, Thera proper, which has a population of around 5000. A much smaller island, Therasia, situated to the northwest, has only two villages. The third portion, Aspronisi, is an uninhabited white fragment. Viewed from the air these three pieces of land still show the circular outline of the former island, but the central area is now a deep bay. Towering cliffs form an inner rim around this expanse of sea, dropping steeply into the water as if sliced through by some gigantic knife. In the center of the bay a dark dome broods and smolders, a constant reminder that Thera is the only active volcano in the Aegean Sea.

The island has probably had a very long history of volcanic disturbance, but geological evidence suggests that the eruption, or series of eruptions, that tore out the center of the island and created the bay may well have been the greatest the world has ever known. It began with a burst of pumice, which built up to a height of 12 feet in some parts of the island. Then there was probably a period of quiescence, followed by another enormous outburst, which covered the island and a vast surrounding area in a mass of fine white ash known as *tephra*. On parts of Thera this tephra is over 200 feet thick. Once the vast magma chamber beneath the earth's crust had ejected this material, its roof—the island of Thera—collapsed, and part of it fell into the sea, forming the central, sea-filled bay known to scientists as a *caldera*.

We can gain some idea of the appalling, widespread devastation caused by such an eruption from eye-witness accounts of a similar event in 1883. In May of that year the island of Krakatoa —a volcano of the same type as Thera—began erupting. Krakatoa is situated in the Sunda Strait, between Java and Sumatra, close to a main sea route between the China Sea and the Indian Ocean. There were therefore a number of ships in the vicinity at the time of the eruption, and their crews were able to give first-hand accounts of it. Krakatoa was uninhabited, and had been dormant for about 200 years, but the 1883 outbreak was preceded by six or seven years of severe earthquakes. Then, on May 20, 1883, the volcano began erupting with booming explosions that rattled doors and windows 100 miles away. Two days later a column of dust and vapor was seen rising from the island to an estimated height of seven miles, and falls of dust were recorded 300 miles away. Observers who landed on the island a week later found it covered by a thin layer of white ash, and the trees stripped of branches by the falling pumice. Activity continued throughout June and July, and at the beginning of August another visitor to Krakatoa reported that all vegetation had been completely destroyed. The climax came on August 26 and 27, beginning with a black, billowing cloud that rose to a height of 17 miles. Violent explosions were heard throughout Java, and warm pumice fell onto ships in the area. During the night of the 26th the crew of the ship *Charles Bal*, sailing about 15 miles east of Krakatoa, saw "balls of white fire" rolling down the rim of the island. The air became hot and choking with a sulfurous smell,

Above: dust and vapor rising from Krakatoa at an early stage of the catastrophic eruption that took place in 1883. This drawing shows the scene on May 27, seven days after the eruption began. It did not reach its climax until August 27 when, early in the morning, four terrific detonations took place, which were so severe that they were heard as far as 3000 miles away and their repercussions were felt on the other side of the world. The island of Krakatoa subsequently collapsed, leaving a submerged caldera similar to that of the Aegean island of Thera.

and the sky was "one second intense blackness, the next a blaze of fire." Throughout the night the noise was so great that the inhabitants of western Java could not sleep. Krakatoa quietened a little toward dawn but early on the morning of the 27th there were four stupendous eruptions, the third of which was heard on the island of Rodriguez, 3000 miles away, and was the loudest noise ever recorded on earth. A cloud of dust rose 50 miles, dispersing its contents over a huge area. An estimated five cubic miles of material was blown out of the volcano, and two thirds of it fell within a 10-mile radius, piling white tephra to a height of 185 feet on the parts of Krakatoa that had survived the devastation. The rest of the ejected material caused a pall of darkness that rapidly spread, reaching Bandong, 150 miles away, late on the same day. Wind-borne dust was still falling 12 days later at a distance of 3300 miles.

Blast waves from the great explosion shattered windows and broke walls up to 100 miles away and were detected all over the globe. But it was the ensuing tidal wave that caused the greatest destruction. In areas bordering the Sunda Strait, 300 towns and villages were destroyed and 36,380 people died as a giant wave ripped through their lands. Tides rose steeply on shores as much as 7000 miles away, and a slight rise was recorded as far away as the English Channel. Sea-borne pumice floated over scores of thousands of square miles, and large amounts were reported all over the Indian Ocean for many months after the eruptions. For many months, too, people all around the world saw the strange phenomena created by dust retained in the upper atmosphere—the sun rose green and then turned blue, the moon was green or blue, and glorious sunsets and afterglows set the sky ablaze.

When visitors ventured to the island after this great cataclysm they found that the northern part of Krakatoa had collapsed

Below left: the eastern Mediterranean, showing the extent of the layer of *tephra* or ash produced by the Thera eruption. The map is based on the geological evidence of sediment cores from the seabed. Below: this map shows the effects of the Krakatoa eruption of 1883: ash falls were reported within the triangular area, and the enormous explosion was heard as far away as the dashed line.

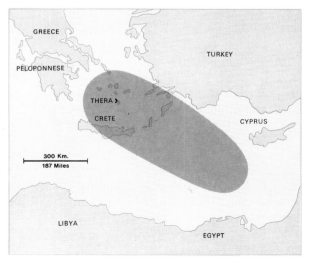

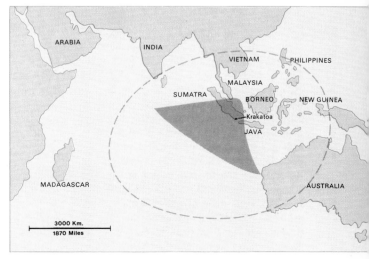

127

Top: the volcanic caldera of
Thera, with the volcanic cones of
Nea Kameni and Palaea Kameni in
its center. The caldera is deeper
than Krakatoa, and four times
as large. Comparison with Krakatoa indicates that the destruction
caused by the Thera eruption and
its effects must have been immense.
Above: an eruption of Nea Kameni
in 1866. Scientific investigations
on Thera following this eruption
proved for the first time when the
caldera must have been formed.

into the sea, creating a caldera, and the remainder of the island
had been split in half.

How does the Thera eruption compare with the paroxysm of
Krakatoa? The Thera caldera is deeper than that formed in
Krakatoa, and its surface area is four times as large. Although
this does not mean that the Thera eruption was four times as
powerful, the structure of the caldera and the extent of the pumice
deposits at Thera indicate that the eruption there was at least as
violent as, and probably even more destructive than, that of
Krakatoa.

Pumice dust from Thera, mixed with lime, produces a very
durable cement, and during the 1860s Therasia provided vast
quantities of pumice for the construction of the Suez Canal and
the new harbor in Port Said. In the course of the quarrying
operations, engineers found themselves hindered by numerous
stone blocks that marked the lower limit of the pumice. These
were the tops of ancient walls buried by fallout from the great
eruption, and they might well have been destroyed in the
interests of commerce had it not been for another eruption,
which began in 1866 and brought a group of scientific observers
to the island. As a result of their interest in the ancient walls,
excavations were begun, notably by the French vulcanologist
Ferdinand Fouqué, who went on to uncover part of a Bronze
Age settlement in Akrotiri in northeast Therasia. Fouqué was
the first to provide evidence that Thera had suffered its dramatic
volcanic collapse sometime in the Bronze Age, 3000 to 1000 B.C.

Fouqué's finds were made before Sir Arthur Evans uncovered
the glories of the Minoan civilization on Crete, and their full
significance was not realized for a long time afterward. Indeed
100 years were to pass before Professor Marinatos began important new excavations in Akrotiri. In the meantime, however,
Thera was not entirely neglected. In 1956 a severe earthquake
disturbed the lower strata of a quarry on the main island of
Thera, exposing the ruins of an ancient building. Human bones,
teeth, and charred wood were found nearby and a Greek
seismologist, Dr. Angelos Galanopoulos, arranged for these to
be submitted to the carbon-14 dating test, which gives the ap-
proximate age of an object by detecting when it "died" and
stopped absorbing carbon from the atmosphere. This showed
the relics to be about 3500 years old. Further tests of this kind
carried out in 1967 on a variety of objects found on Thera have
enabled scholars to put the date of the Thera eruption at between
1500 and 1450 B.C. And that coincides with the period when the
great Minoan civilization suddenly declined.

In his book *The End of Atlantis*, a scholarly study of the
Atlantis legend, Professor J. V. Luce discusses the effects of the
Thera eruption on Crete: "We do not know what happened on
Crete and on the islands and coasts of the Aegean, but I consider
it a safe guess that the loss of life and damage to property were
no less [than from Krakatoa]. They may well have been many
times as great. We can say with reasonable assurance that Crete
had ceased to be a great maritime power after the middle of the
15th century B.C. Is it not reasonable to suppose that the Thera
eruption was a major factor in her downfall?"

Supporting evidence for this point of view has come from cores of sediment taken from the floor of the Eastern Mediterranean. It was published in 1965 by two American scientists, D. Ninkovich and B. C. Heezen of the Lamont Geological Observatory, Columbia University, who concluded from the distribution of the volcanic ash found in these deposits that the Thera explosion was a major catastrophe for Minoan Crete. In their opinion, this catastrophe led directly to a transference of power in the area from the Minoans to the mainland Greeks—the Mycenaeans.

The remarkable buildings, frescoes, and pottery found on Thera indicate that it was part of the Minoan island empire. Discussing the 1967 excavations made by Professor Marinatos in Akrotiri, J. V. Luce comments: "Enough evidence has been accumulated for us to say with some assurance that the settlement has distinctly Minoan features, and was clearly in close contact with Crete. It is likely to have been a Minoan colony or dependency, possibly the seat of the Minoan ruler of the island."

Luce, like a number of other scholars who have studied the exciting finds on Thera and Crete, believes that Plato's Atlantis story is a composite picture of the Minoan downfall. The "disappearance" of Atlantis is really the sudden fall from power

of the Minoans, coupled with the cataclysmic events on part of their island empire. Luce remarks that he does not look for the lost Atlantis under the surface of Thera bay. "For me 'lost Atlantis' is a historical rather than a geographical concept."

Greek seismologist Dr. Angelos Galanopoulos takes a more literal view of the legend, and has gone a long way toward satisfying many critics of the Atlantis-in-the-Aegean theory with an ingenious hypothesis. Galanopoulos interprets Plato's story as a description of two islands. The larger is the "royal state"—Crete. The smaller is the metropolis, or capital city and religious center—Thera. Plato says that the metropolis of Atlantis was about 11 miles in diameter. This is the same as the former size of Thera. But Galanopoulos noted that other measurements in

Plato's account seemed to be far too great in comparison. However, he found that if all measurements over 1000 were divided by 10, they would neatly reduce Atlantis to a size consistent with that of the Minoan empire. Therefore Galanopoulos argued that at some time a tenfold error had crept into the Atlantis story—either when the Egyptians recorded it, or after they gave the story to Solon, who handed it down through a number of generations. Galanopoulos believes that in the translation of Egyptian scripts by Solon, or possibly of Minoan scripts from which the Egyptians obtained the story, the symbol for 100 was rendered as 1000. A modern example of this sort of confusion is the difference between the American billion, which is one thousand millions, and the English billion, which is one million millions.

This mistake, if it occurred, would affect not only the size of Atlantis and its population but also the date of its destruction. Take off the final zero in Plato's figures over 1000, says Galanopoulos, and we find that the date of the submergence of Atlantis coincides with that of the Thera eruption. Instead of sinking 9000 years before Solon's visit to Egypt—a date that caused most people to dismiss the account as a myth because there is no evidence of an advanced civilization existing at such an early period—Atlantis disappeared only 900 years before Solon's trip. Because Solon's journey took place around 600 B.C., this would mean that Atlantis was destroyed around 1500 B.C.— just when the experts believe Thera erupted and Crete suffered its downfall.

Galanopoulos first put forward his hypothesis in 1960, and it is interesting to recall that the 1500 B.C. date for the destruction of Atlantis had already been suggested 10 years earlier by Immanuel Velikovsky in his book *Worlds in Collision*. Writing before the present Atlantis–Thera–Crete theory had evolved, Velikovsky also believed that there was one zero too many in Plato's date.

If Atlantis was in the Aegean, why did Plato apparently situate it in the distant Atlantic Ocean? And why, if Atlantis sank so close to the Greek mainland, were the Greeks so vague about its

Above: a vase of flowers, a fresco discovered in 1972-3 on the wall of the so-called West House on Thera. The beauty and originality of the paintings discovered on Thera have astonished the world, and the discovery of such sophisticated artifacts on the island helps support the argument advanced by Dr. Angelos Galanopoulos, that Thera-Crete composed Atlantis, and that Thera was the chief town.

Left: the U.S. oceanographic research vessel *Chain*. In 1966, James W. Mavor used the *Chain* to make sonar soundings of the seabed in the sunken caldera of Thera in an attempt to prove Galanopoulos's theory. He hoped to find evidence of the existence of the harbors and canals described by Plato in his account of Atlantis, but although his voyage added considerably to knowledge of the caldera, and of the volcanic deposits on the seabed, no new evidence to prove the Thera-Atlantis theory emerged. Right: fresco found on Thera, of a young woman, the "priestess." Such sophisticated art is common to Thera, Crete—and Plato's Atlantis.

existence, having to rely on the Egyptians for information about the "lost continent"?

It has been suggested that Plato placed Atlantis in the Atlantic simply because, according to his figures, it was too big to fit anywhere else. Alternatively, there is the possibility of yet another misinterpretation originating with Solon. Plato's account states that Atlantis lay "beyond the Pillars of Hercules"—the name given to the Strait of Gibraltar in Plato's time. Thus his readers automatically assumed that Atlantis was in the Atlantic. But Dr. Galanopoulos has pointed out that the name "Pillars of Hercules" was also once applied to two promontories on the south coast of Greece (ancient Mycenae), facing Crete. If Plato's account refers to these, says Galanopoulos, then the Minoans are almost certainly the Atlanteans.

Archaeological evidence shows that the Minoan culture began to acquire strong Mycenaean characteristics around the time of its downfall, and that the Minoans were starting to lose their dominance of the Aegean. The Minoans and the Mycenaeans may well have been rivals, just as Plato described the Athenians and the Atlanteans to be. Whether the Mycenaeans had conquered parts of Crete, or whether the two cultures underwent a more peaceful integration, discoveries in Knossos show that, after the fall of Crete, the Mycenaeans took the Minoans' place as the major force in the Aegean. The Mycenaeans would even appear to have taken control of the palace in Knossos, which, though damaged, had survived because it was inland.

The Greeks, however, were still too young a people to recall the history of these events with any clarity, though with hindsight we can find some of the story in their legends. J. V. Luce comments that, "The Greeks remembered very little at all about the 15th century B.C. Their national consciousness was then only in an early formative stage. Their main saga cycles date from the 13th century when, under the leadership of Mycenae, they had become a major power in the eastern Mediterranean." Luce adds that "even the Mycenaean world as a whole was only dimly remembered by the later Greeks." The Egyptians, a much older race, had long been trading with the Minoans and recorded the visits of Minoans to Egypt. So it is perhaps not surprising if the Egyptians knew more than the Greeks themselves about their talented forebears.

According to Plato, the Egyptian priests told Solon: "You remember only one deluge though there have been many, and you do not know that the finest and best race of men that ever existed lived in your country; you and your fellow citizens are descended from the few survivors who remained, but you know nothing about it, because of the many intervening generations silent for lack of written speech."

In the opinion of some scholars, that quotation supplies further evidence for the Atlantis-in-the-Aegean theory, and for the Egyptian origin of the Atlantis story. The Egyptians are apparently referring to a literacy gap that has since been confirmed. Scripts known as Linear A and B were used in Crete, Greece, and the Aegean islands during the second millennium B.C., but they disappeared from use after 1200 B.C. They do not appear to have been replaced by any other form of writing until around 850 B.C.,

Above: fresco of a coastal city, with ships offshore, from the West House on Thera. The city is surrounded by seas full of fish; on land deer run among the burgeoning trees. What other picture could so closely represent Plato's ocean-ringed land of milk and honey as this painting by an unknown Theran of long ago?

when the Greek archaic script appeared. So it seems that, even had there been any local records of the Thera explosion and the fall of Crete, they would have been written in a language that the Greeks of Plato's time would not have understood.

As a result of the discoveries in the Aegean, a number of scholars are now prepared to believe not only that Plato's account is based on historical reality, but that it is an astonishingly accurate record of events that occurred over 1000 years before he wrote his story. Until further information about the Minoan culture emerges, however, even the Atlantis-in-the-Aegean theory is open to different interpretations. Professor Galanopoulos, for example, believes that Thera was as important to the Minoans as Crete was. He regards Thera as the center of Minoan life and Crete as its larger adjunct. Galanopoulos pictures the slopes of the small volcanic island teeming with life and adorned with the white temples and palaces of a majestic city. When the eruption came, these great feats of architecture—equal to those discovered on Crete—would have been buried in fallout, then submerged beneath the waters that now fill the Thera basin.

Attempts to detect submerged harbors and canals at Thera similar to those described by Plato have been made, using the latest sonar equipment. In 1966 Dr. James W. Mavor of the Woods Hole Oceanographic Institution was given permission to carry out runs across the bay with the research vessel *Chain*.

The findings of the *Chain* are related in Mavor's book *Voyage to Atlantis*. Although they have added to our understanding of the shape and depth of the caldera and the volcanic deposits beneath the sea, they could not provide the evidence needed to support Galanopoulos's theory.

Clearly there is a need for deep-sea diving equipment to be used in the Thera basin, and in 1975 it was announced that the French underwater explorer Jacques Cousteau had received permission to dive and carry out research in the area. Cousteau was reported to be planning a year-long study off Thera and Delos (another island in the Cyclades), which would be recorded on film for television, and his research vessel was said to have been fitted with special "treasure-hunting" gear, including two lateral sonars that can scan the seabed for over 400 yards on either side of the ship. Speaking of Thera, Cousteau is quoted as saying: "This is the best contender for the title of the real Atlantis. We know there is something down there under the waves. We are determined to find out what."

Pending the discovery of new evidence, no one can say for sure that the Atlantis mystery has been solved. But excavations now in progress may soon be able to show whether the Minoans—possibly the most accomplished and inventive race the world has ever known—were not only the forefathers of Greek civilization, and ultimately of Europe, but also the lost and fabled Atlanteans.

8

The Mystery Deepens

In 1968 two commercial airline pilots flying over the Bahamas spotted what appeared to be several underwater buildings coming to the surface. The pilots made their sighting just off the coast of Bimini and photographed the underwater formations from the air. Their discovery was immediately hailed by some as the fulfillment of a 28-year-old prophecy concerning the reappearance of Atlantis. Indeed one of the pilots had been keeping a lookout for underwater structures while flying his regular assignments because he believed Atlantis was about to reemerge from the Atlantic in this very area.

The man concerned is a member of the

"Thera may yet have a rival for the title of Atlantis"

Association for Research and Enlightenment, an organization based in Virginia Beach, Virginia, which is dedicated to the study of the teachings and "psychic readings" of the late Edgar Cayce, the "sleeping prophet" and psychic healer. Between 1923 and 1944 Cayce made numerous references to Atlantis in the course of trance interviews concerning the alleged former lives of the people who consulted him. These interviews were recorded verbatim, and much of the material about Atlantis has been published in a book called *Edgar Cayce on Atlantis*, by Cayce's son Edgar Evans Cayce. It includes this prediction, made in June 1940: "Poseidia will be among the first portions of Atlantis to rise again. Expect it in '68 and '69; not so far away!"

According to the Cayce readings, Poseidia was the "western section of Atlantis," and the area off Bimini is the highest point of this sunken land. So the ARE is naturally delighted about the underwater find in the Bahamas, just where and when the famous prophet said something would appear. Until this and similar discoveries have been thoroughly explored, we have to admit that Thera may yet have an equally plausible rival for the title of Atlantis, right where most people always considered the long-lost continent to be—in the Atlantic.

In his book *The Mystery of Atlantis* Charles Berlitz comments that: "Other underwater ruins have subsequently been found near other Caribbean islands, including what appears to be an entire city submerged off the coast of Haiti, and still another at the bottom of a lake. What appears to be an underwater road (or perhaps a series of plazas or foundations) was discovered in 1968 off north Bimini beneath several fathoms of water. From these numerous findings, it would appear that part of the continental shelf of the Atlantic and Caribbean was once dry land, sunk or flooded during a period when man was already civilized."

Not everyone accepts these underwater features as being of man-made origin. The so-called "Bimini road" is dismissed by skeptics as nothing more than beach rock that just happens to have produced an unusual effect. Berlitz and Dr Manson Valentine, the American archaeologist and oceanographer who discovered the "road," do not agree. "It should be pointed out," writes Berlitz, "that beach rock does not form great blocks which fit together in a pattern, that haphazardly splitting rock does not make 90-degree turns, nor does it normally have regularly laid-out passageways running between sections of it. Nor, above all, are 'natural' beach rocks, lying on the ocean floor, likely to be found supported by stone pillars precisely placed beneath them!"

Other sightings made off Bimini, at distances up to 100 miles from the shore, include what appear to be vertical walls, a great arch, and pyramids or bases for pyramids under the sea. Some 10 miles north of Andros, another island in the Bahamas, pilots have photographed formations on the seabed that look like great circles of standing stones, reminiscent of Stonehenge. Off the coasts of eastern Yucatán and British Honduras seemingly man-made roads stretch far out to sea, and off Venezuela a 100-mile "wall" runs along the ocean bottom. However, geologists have declared many of these to be natural features, and deem the Venezuelan wall "too big to be considered man-

Below: a diver taking part in ARE's Poseidia 75 expedition to Bimini in the Bahamas examines an encrusted marble column found about a mile south of the Bimini Road. Medical clairvoyant Edgar Cayce, who made predictions about Atlantis, foretold that the western part of the continent would rise from the sea in 1968 or 1969. In 1968, what appeared to be a vast underwater road was discovered off Bimini, and the next year the columns, of which this is one, were found.

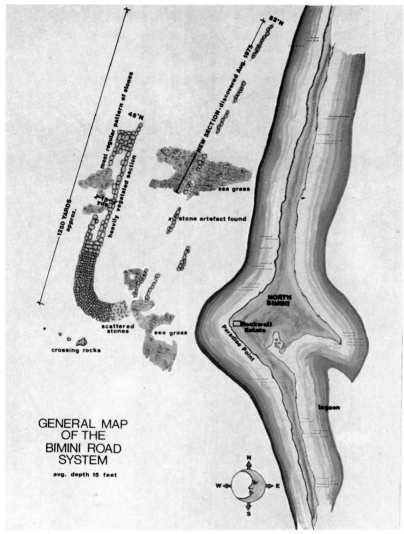

GENERAL MAP
OF THE
BIMINI ROAD
SYSTEM
avg. depth 15 feet

Left: map of the Bimini Road drawn after aerial and underwater surveys carried out by the Poseidia 75 expedition. The road is magnified to approximately twice its actual size in relation to the island of Bimini. Shaped roughly like a letter J, it is some three quarters of a mile long and composed of huge stone blocks, often 15 feet square. On this map, the X marking the discovery of a stone artifact relates to a fragment of what appeared to be tongue-and-groove masonry discovered on the Poseidia 75 expedition by one of its members, Dr. David Zink.

Below: aerial view of part of the Bimini Road, photographed from beyond the curve of the "J"—in the background is Paradise Point on the island of Bimini. Those who support the man-made road theory argue that the stones could not have been arranged as they are without human intervention, particularly as they are of a different rock type from the seabed beneath. Skeptics believe, however, that the "road" is a natural rock formation, albeit an unusual one.

made." According to Berlitz, the Russians have explored an underwater building complex covering over 10 acres of the sea floor north of Cuba, and the French bathyscaphe *Archimède* has reported sighting flights of steps carved in the steep continental shelf off northern Puerto Rico.

Do these intriguing finds indicate that Atlantis was, after all, in the Atlantic? It seems we must keep an open mind until they have been investigated more thoroughly. Meanwhile, let us take a fresh look at the Atlantic Ocean to see if the theory of continental drift might still leave room for a missing continent there. When a computer was used to reassemble the continental jigsaw, the fit across the Atlantic was found, with some adjustment, to be fairly satisfactory. But that picture does not take account of a fascinating underwater feature known as the mid-Atlantic Ridge. This mountainous ridge, nearly two miles high and hundreds of miles wide, runs in an S-curve down the Atlantic midway between the Americas and Africa and Europe, following the contours of those continents and marking its course above water with a number of islands, such as the Azores, Ascension Island, and Tristan da Cunha.

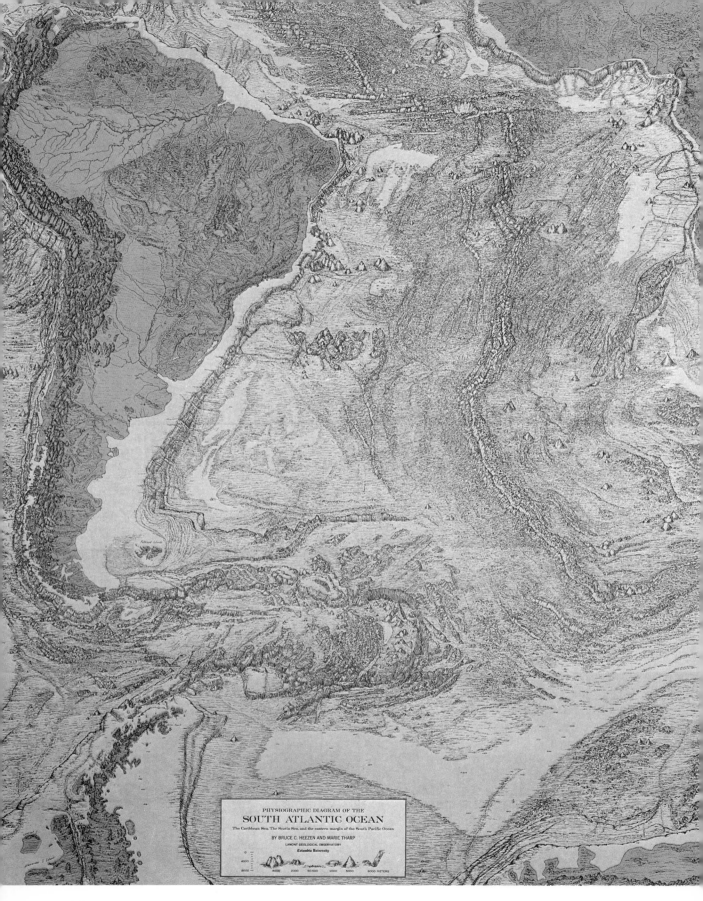

PHYSIOGRAPHIC DIAGRAM OF THE

SOUTH ATLANTIC OCEAN

The Caribbean Sea, The Scotia Sea, and the eastern margin of the South Pacific Ocean

BY BRUCE C. HEEZEN AND MARIE THARP

LAMONT GEOLOGICAL OBSERVATORY

Columbia University

Left: diagram of the physical features underlying the Atlantic Ocean. The mid-Atlantic Ridge curves from north to south down the middle of the ocean. Atlantist Ignatius Donnelly suggested that the ridge might be a remnant of the sunken continent of Atlantis, but scientific opinion today holds that, rather than being formed above the surface of the waters and sinking, it was in fact pushed up from beneath the ocean floor. Recent research does seem to indicate that there is a sunken continent in the Atlantic, lying between Africa and South America, but this continent sank long before man's appearance on earth.

Below: the French bathyscaphe *Archimède*. The crew of *Archimède* produced what could be fresh evidence to support the existence of a sunken continent in the Caribbean area when they reported seeing flights of steps carved in the continental shelf off the island of Puerto Rico.

As early as 1883 Ignatius Donnelly suggested that the mid-Atlantic Ridge was a remnant of Atlantis. But most modern geologists and oceanographers consider that, far from being the relic of a continent that sank beneath the sea, the ridge was forced upward from the ocean floor, probably by volcanic activity. One theory is that as the continents drifted apart they produced a huge fault line that is a center of earthquake and volcanic action. Some of the earth's molten center has erupted through this crack and built up into a ridge, even rising above the waves in several places. However, there is evidence that this explanation may have to be reviewed before too long.

Seabed cores taken from the mid-Atlantic Ridge in 1957 brought up freshwater plants from a depth of two miles. And in one of the deep valleys, known as Romanche, sands have been found that appear to have been formed by weathering when that part of the ridge was above water level. In 1969 a Duke University research expedition dredged 50 sites along an underwater ridge running from Venezuela to the Virgin Islands, and brought up granitic rocks, which are normally found only on continents. Commenting on this discovery, Dr. Bruce Heezen of the Lamont Geological Observatory said: "Up to now, geologists generally believed that light granitic or acid igneous rocks are confined to the continents and that the crust of the earth beneath the sea is composed of heavier, dark-colored basaltic rock. . . . Thus, the occurrence of light-colored granitic rocks may support an old theory that a continent formerly existed in the region of the eastern Caribbean and that these rocks may represent the core of a subsided, lost continent."

A recent report on the nature of the Atlantic seabed appears to confirm that there is at least part of a former continent lying beneath the ocean. Under the headline "Concrete Evidence for Atlantis?" the British journal *New Scientist* of June 5, 1975 reported: "Although they make no such fanciful claim from their results as to have discovered the mythical mid-Atlantic landmass, an international group of oceanographers has now convincingly confirmed preliminary findings that a sunken block of continent lies in the middle of the Atlantic Ocean. The discovery comes from analyzing dredge samples taken along the line of the Vema offset fault, a long east-west fracture zone lying between Africa and South America close to latitude 11°N."

The report goes on to state that in 1971 two researchers from the University of Miami recovered some shallow-water limestone fragments from deep water in the area. Minerals in the limestone indicated that they came from a nearby source of granite that was unlikely to occur on the ocean floor. More exhaustive analysis of the dredge samples revealed that the limestones included traces of shallow-water fossils, implying formation in very shallow water indeed, a view confirmed by the ratios of oxygen and carbon isotopes found in the fragments. One piece of limestone was pitted and showed evidence of tidal action.

The researchers believe that the limestone dates from the Mesozoic era (between 70 and 220 million years ago) and forms a cap "on a residual continental block left behind as the Atlantic spread out into an ocean." The *New Scientist* observes that "the granitic minerals could thus have come from the bordering

Above: volcanic eruption on Surtsey, just south of Iceland. Atlantists believe that recorded changes in the physical features of the Atlantic Ocean caused by volcanic eruptions provide ample evidence for siting the lost Atlantis in the Atlantic. Volcanic activity not only explains how the continent might have disappeared, but also explains it in exactly the way Plato described.

continents while the ocean was still in its infancy. Vertical movements made by the block appear to have raised it above sea level at some period during its history."

It would therefore seem that there *is* a lost continent in the Atlantic, but unfortunately for Atlantists, it evidently disappeared long before man appeared on earth. Most scientists remain convinced that there is no likelihood of finding the Atlantis described by Plato in the area of the mid-Atlantic Ridge. As L. Sprague de Camp comments in his *Lost Continents*, nearly all of the ridge, except for the small and mountainous Azores region, is under two or three miles of water, "and there is no known way to get a large island down to that depth in anything like the 10,000 years required to fit in with Plato's date for the sinking of Atlantis." He also points to a report published in 1967 by Dr. Maurice Ewing of Columbia University, who announced that "after 13 years of exploring the mid-Atlantic Ridge," he had "found no trace of sunken cities."

Atlantists reply that Dr. Ewing could have been looking in the wrong places, or perhaps too close to the center of the destructive forces that plunged Atlantis into the ocean. Some Atlantists have suggested that the original Atlantic landmass broke up into at least two parts, one of which sank long after the other. Perhaps Plato's Atlantis was a remnant of the continent that oceanographers now appear to have detected in the Atlantic, and perhaps it was not submerged until very much more recent times. The bed of the Atlantic is, after all, an unstable area and one that has given birth to numerous islands, then swallowed them up again. In 1811, for example, volcanic activity in the Azores resulted in the emergence of a new island called Sambrina, which shortly sank back again into the sea. In our own time, the island of Surtsey, 20 miles southwest of Iceland has slowly risen from the ocean. Surtsey was formed during a continuous underwater eruption between 1963 and 1966.

If Atlantis did exist in the Atlantic above the great fault line that runs between the present continents, it would certainly have been plagued by earthquakes and volcanic eruptions. Is it mere coincidence that Plato should have situated his lost continent in an ocean that does apparently contain such a continent, and in an area subject to the very kind of catastrophe he describes? Atlantists think not.

On the other hand, there are some Atlantists who believe that the destruction of Atlantis was brought about not by geological events but by a man-made disaster, such as a nuclear explosion. According to the Cayce readings the Atlanteans achieved an astonishingly high level of technology before the continent sank, around 10,000 B.C. They invented the laser, aircraft, television, death rays, atomic energy, and cybernetic control of human beings, and it was the misuse of the tremendously powerful natural forces they had developed that caused their destruction.

Cayce is best-known for his apparent ability to diagnose illness even in people whom he had never met. This ability was tested by a group of physicians from Hopkinsville and Bowling Green, Kentucky. They discovered that when Cayce was in a state of trance, it was sufficient to give him the name and address of a patient for him to supply a wealth of information about that person, often drawing attention to medical conditions of which the physicians were then unaware, but that subsequent tests on the patient proved to be correct. This work alone would appear to justify the description of Cayce as America's most talented psychic. And if one aspect of his clairvoyant powers could prove so successful, it seems reasonable to give a fair hearing to other psychic statements he made, however fantastic.

Cayce's sons, who help run the organization set up to study his work, admit that their life would be far simpler if Edgar Cayce had never mentioned Atlantis. Hugh Lynn Cayce comments: "It would be very easy to present a very tight evidential picture of Edgar Cayce's psychic ability and the helpfulness of his readings if we selected only those which are confirmed and completely validated. This would not be fair in a total, overall evaluation of his life's work. My brother and I know that Edgar Cayce did not read Plato's material on Atlantis, or books on Atlantis, and that he, so far as we know, had absolutely no knowledge of this subject. If his unconscious fabricated this material or wove it together from existing legends and writings, we believe that it is the most amazing example of a telepathic-clairvoyant scanning of existing legends and stories in print or of the minds of persons dealing with the Atlantis theory." Edgar Evans Cayce makes the comment that "unless proof of the existence of Atlantis is one day discovered, Edgar Cayce is in a very unenviable position. On the other hand, if he proves accurate on this score he may become as famous an archaeologist or historian as he was a medical clairvoyant."

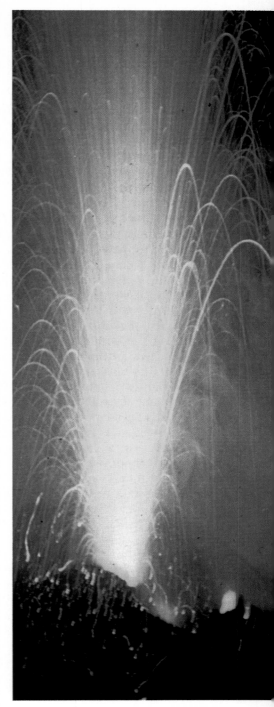

Above: volcanic eruption in the Lipari Islands, off southwestern Italy. The volcanic activity explanation for Atlantis's disappearance could support a Mediterranean Atlantis as effectively as an Atlantic one. Volcanic eruptions also occur in the Mediterranean, and in the Thera caldera they have created totally new islands.

If, as his sons and thousands of followers believe, Edgar Cayce's readings were supernormal, and not the product of reading the works of others, it is certainly an intriguing case. There are, for example, some fascinating similarities between Cayce's descriptions of Atlantis and those of occultists such as Madame Blavatsky, Rudolf Steiner, and W. Scott-Elliot, including references to the Atlanteans' telepathic and other supernormal powers, their advanced technology, their moral disintegration, and the civil strife and misuse of their powers that finally caused their demise. Cayce's readings also mention Lemuria, or Mu. Either Cayce was psychically reading the works of these earlier writers, or he—and they—really were "tuning in" to the past.

Whatever the result of future investigations around the splendid temples and palaces of Crete, or in the depths of the Thera basin, there will still be people who continue to look for Atlantis in the Atlantic Ocean. Scholars may have made out a convincing case for the identification of Plato's Atlantis with the Minoan civilization of the Aegean, but their opponents argue that the existence of such a civilization—however striking its similarities with Atlantis—does not preclude the existence of an even greater civilization in the Atlantic. The finds in the Bahamas remain to be verified, and the discovery of what appears to be a submerged continent in the Atlantic adds a new dimension to the Atlantis mystery.

Whatever prompted Plato to write about Atlantis, he could never have dreamed that he would start a worldwide quest for the lost continent. Perhaps, as his pupil Aristotle hinted, "he who invented it also destroyed it." Yet through a fortuitous accident—or a canny understanding of the human spirit—Plato hit upon a story that has struck a responsive chord in people's minds and hearts down the centuries. Whether his story was fact or fiction, a distorted version of real events or a fable that just happened to tie in with reality, it has managed to enchant, baffle, and challenge mankind for over 2000 years.

The persistence of the Atlantis legend is almost as intriguing as the lost continent itself. What is it that keeps the Atlantis debate alive? Is it a longing for reassurance that men and women once knew the secret of happiness, and really did inhabit a Garden of Eden? Is it the thrill of the search—the hope of finding a master key to unlock the secrets of the past? Or is it simply man's thirst for mystery itself—for something grand and inexplicable, larger than himself? Certainly popular interest in the mystical side of Atlantis is always most intense when the life of the spirit is in greatest disarray—during the latter half of the 19th century, in the aftermath of Darwin's bombshell, for example, and during our own time.

The day may yet come when the key is found and the mystery of Atlantis is solved once and for all. The solution may be simple or complex. It could be sensational or disappointingly dull. We may already suspect the answer, or it may surprise us. Either way, it would rob the world of one of its most fascinating enigmas. Atlantis has intrigued and inspired people for a very long time. Perhaps, for the time being, we should be glad that the answer has not yet been found, and that Plato's lost continent remains just beyond our grasp.

Right: the fisher, a fresco from the West House on Thera. The evidence seems to point to Thera as the origin of Plato's Atlantis, but the mystery still lingers, for the evidence is not yet conclusive. Until new discoveries are made, or fresh proof uncovered, we can pursue our quest for the lost utopia. We can wonder whether this fisherboy is really an Atlantean.

142

143

Picture Credits

2	The Tate Gallery, London/Photo John Webb © Aldus Books
4	Museo Pio Clementino, Vatican/Scala, Florence
7	Museo Nazionale, Naples/Scala, Florence
9(T)	Photo J.-L. Charmet
9(B)	Nasjonalgalleriet, Oslo
10(T)	Museo Pio Clementino, Vatican/Scala, Florence
11	Stanze di Raffaello, Vatican/Scala, Florence
12(T)	The Ny Carlsberg Glyptothek, Copenhagen
12(B)	Hirmer Fotoarchiv, München
13	Photo Peter Clayton
14	National Museum, Athens/Scala, Florence
15—17	Bruno Elletori © Aldus Books
18	The Tate Gallery, London/Photo John Webb © Aldus Books
19(L)	Louvre/Giraudon
19(R)	The Mansell Collection, London
20	Reproduced by courtesy of the Trustees of the British Museum
21(T)	Photo Dr. Ernst Meyer from Schliemann Briefwechsel I
21(B)	Hirmer Fotoarchiv, München
22(T)	Barnaby's Picture Library
22(B)	Ashmolean Museum, Oxford
23(B)	The Trustees of Sir Arthur Evans
24	Aldus Archives
25(B)	Courtesy of the Association for Research and Enlightenment, Virginia
27	Robert Harding Associates
28	Brown Brothers
29(R), 30(L)	Aldus Archives
30(R)	National Portrait Gallery, London
31	Photo J.-L. Charmet
33(TL)(BL)	Minnesota Historical Society
33(TR)(BR)	Aldus Archives
34	Michael Holford Library photo
35(TR)	Aldus Archives
35(B)	Camer and Pen
36(L)	Michael Holford Library photo
36(B)	Aldus Archives
37(T)	Minnesota Historical Society
37(B)	Victoria & Albert Museum, London/Photo Eileen Tweedy © Aldus Books
38	Glasgow Herald
39(TL)	©Aldus Books
39(TR)	Zdenek Burian
39(B)	Abbé H. Breuil, 400,000 Years of Cave Art, © Fernand Windels, 1952
40(T)	Alan Hollingbery © Aldus Books
40(B)	Culver Pictures
41	Universitätsbibliothek, Heidelberg. Cod.Pal.Germ.60, fol.179v
42(T)	© Aldus Books
42(B)	Reproduced by courtesy of the Trustees of the British Museum
43	Aldus Archives
44	Reproduced by courtesy of the
45	Trustees of the British Museum Aldus Archives
47	Robert Harding Associates
48	Aldus Archives
49(TR)(B)	Werner Forman Archive
50(L)	National Museum of Anthropology, Mexico City, from Mexican Art, The Hamlyn Group/Photo Constantino Reyes-Valerio
50—51(TC)	Bodleian Library, Oxford
50(B)	Museo Histórico Regional del Cuzco, Calle Heladeros, Peru
51(R)	Michael Holford Library photo
52(TL)	Reproduced by courtesy of the Trustees of the British Museum
52(B)	Paul Popper Ltd.
53(T)	Keystone
54—55(T)	From photos in the possession of Brian Fawcett
55(B)	From a drawing by Brian Fawcett
56(T)	John H. Moore
56—57(B)	From a photo in the possession of Brian Fawcett
57(T)	Psychic News
58(L)	From Mexican Art, The Hamlyn Group/Photo Constantino Reyes-Valerio
58(R)	Robert Harding Associates
59	Museo Nacional di Antropologia, Mexico
61(T)	Robert Harding Associates
61(BL)	Aldus Archives
61(BR)	Werner Forman Archive
62(B)	Michael Holford Library photo
63	Museo Nacional de Historia, Madrid/Photo Pulido Gudino
65	David South/Camera Press
67(T)	The Parker Gallery, London
67(B)	Musée de l'Homme, Paris
68	Pierre Honoré, In quest of the White God, Hutchinson & Co. Ltd., London, 1963
69	Photo Mas
70	Aldus Archives
71(T)	Photo J.-L. Charmet
71(B), 72(T)	Aldus Archives
73(B)	James Churchward, The Lost Continent of Mu, Neville Spearman Ltd., London, 1942
74(T)	Alan Hollingbery © Aldus Books
75, 77(T)(B)	James Churchward, The Lost Continent of Mu, Neville Spearman Ltd, London, 1942
77(C)	Alan Hollingbery © Aldus Books
78(L)	Robert Harding Associates
79(T)	Camera Press
79(C)	Courtesy The Royal Norwegian Embassy, London
79(B)	William Hodges 1744–1797. Woman of Easter Island. Drawn from nature by W. Hodges. Engraved by J. Caldwell. Line engraving 25.5 × 19.5 cm. (in James Cook, A voyage towards the South Pole and round the world..., London, 1777). From the Rex Nan Kivell Collection in the National Library of Australia
80—81	Photos Thor Heyerdahl
83	Trustees of the British Museum (Natural History)
85	Robert Harding Associates
86	Alan Hollingbery © Aldus Books
87(T)	Heinrich Schmidt, Ernst Haeckel, Frommannsche Buchhandlung, Jena, 1934
87(B)	Mary Evans Picture Library
89	The Mansell Collection, London
91	Peter Tomlin © Aldus Books
92—93	Aldus Archives
94	Radio Times Hulton Picture Library
95—97	Christopher Foss © Aldus Books
99	Laing Art Gallery, Newcastle upon Tyne (Tyne and Wear Museums Service)
101(T)	Werner Forman Archive
101(B)	Sigurgeir Jonasson/Frank W. Lane
102(T)	Laing Art Gallery, Newcastle upon Tyne (Tyne and Wear Museums Service)
102(B)	Alan Hollingbery © Aldus Books
103(B)	Werner Forman Archive
104	Photo Fima Noveck
105(T)	NASA
105(B)	Hale Observatories
106(T)	Alan Hollingbery © Aldus Books
106(C)(B)	Wiener Library
108	The Tate Gallery, London/Photo John Webb © Aldus Books
109(R)	Bodleian Library, Oxford
110(T)	Victoria & Albert Museum, London/Photo Eileen Tweedy © Aldus Books
110(B)	The Mansell Collection, London
112(T)	Else Wegener, Alfred Wegener, 1960, with the permission of F. A Brockhaus, Wiesbaden
113	David Nockels © Aldus Books
114—115	Hawke Studio/Michael Turner © Aldus Books
117	Photo Dimitrios Harissiadis
119(T)	Robert Harding Associates
119(B)—120	Picturepoint, London
121(T)	The Trustees of Sir Arthur Evans
121(B)	Chr. Mathioulakis & N. Gouvoussis, Athens
122	Photo Dimitrios Harissiadis
123(L)	Alan Hollingbery © Aldus Books
123(T)—125	Bruno Elletori © Aldus Books
126	Royal Society Report on Krakatoa, 1889
127(B), 128(T)	Alan Hollingbery © Aldus Books
128(B)	The Mansell Collection, London
129(T)	© G. Goakimedes
129(B)	Associates Press
130(T)	Athens Annals of Archaeology
130(B)	Woods Hole Oceanographic Institution
131—133	Athens Annals of Archaeology
134	Barbara Pfeffer People © Time Inc. 1976
135	Icelandic Photo & Press Service
136	Photo Roger Haydock
137	Photos John Steele
138	Bruce C. Heezen and Marie Tharp, Physiographic Diagram of the South Atlantic Ocean, The Geological Society of America, 1962
139	Keystone
140	Icelandic Photo & Press Service
141	Tomas Micek/Frank W. Lane
143	Athens Annals of Archaeology